On Track to Success in 30 Days

Energize Your Real Estate Career to Become a Top Producer

Carla Cross, CRB

Real Estate Education Company®
a division of Dearborn Financial Publishing, Inc.

Dedication

In memory of my father and mother, Bob and Eleanora Garrison

Acquisitions Editor: Christine E. Litavsky
Managing Editor: Jack Kiburz
Interior Design: Lucy Jenkins
Cover Design: Salvatore Concialdi

© 1996 by Dearborn Financial Publishing, Inc.®

Published by Real Estate Education Company®,
a division of Dearborn Financial Publishing, Inc.®

Printed in the United States of America

98 10 9 8 7 6 5 4 3 2

Library of Congress Cataloging-in-Publication Data

Cross, Carla.
    On track to success in 30 days: energize your real estate career to become a top producer / Carla Cross.
        p.   cm.
    Includes bibliographical references and index.
    ISBN 0-7931-2225-2 (pbk.)
    1. Real estate agents. 2. Real estate business—Vocational guidance. I. Title.
HD1382.C76   1996   96-28255
333.33'023'73—dc20   CIP

Real Estate Education Company books are available at special quantity discounts to use as premiums and sales promotions, or for use in corporate training programs. For more information, please call the Special Sales Manager at 800-621-9621, ext. 4384, or write to Dearborn Financial Publishing, Inc., 155 N. Wacker Drive, Chicago, IL 60606-1719.

Acknowledgments

For me, writing a book is like remembering a favorite tune that I haven't heard for awhile. First, it's hard to remember all the notes of the tune. Then, as I concentrate on it, I remember each of the phrases. The chord progressions come back, and, pretty soon, I'm remembering that tune in its entirety—with all the emotions that go with it. (Remember *your* favorite song and what it means to you?) As I wrote this book, I remembered all the good advice my teachers, coaches, and managers gave me. I remembered all the wonderful REALTORS® I've known, who have, through their efforts, raised the standards of the industry. I not only remembered all these people, I remembered my warm feelings toward them.

To be memorable, a tune must have just the right combination of melody, harmony, and rhythm. It's never a great tune without a masterful blend of all three musical elements. It's the same with a book. To be memorable, it must have the right combination of words, emotions, and organization. In my opinion, this combination is only *organized* by the writer. The material is not really *created* by the author. The material is the result of the contributions of all the people the writer's ever been influenced by.

My thanks, first, to all those influential people—people who, through this book, are passing on their influence to you for your increased success.

In particular, thank you to the exceptional owners, managers, and agents who answered my surveys in preparation for writing this book. You'll read their invaluable advice to you throughout the chapters:

Caroline Ruhl Beason, CRB, president, Ruhl & Ruhl REALTORS®, Inc.; Bettendorf, Iowa. Caroline is a pioneer in searching out and bringing to her associates new business methods.

Sheila Bell, CRB, CRS, GRI, vice president/director of career development, Sibcy Cline REALTORS®, Cincinnati, Ohio. Sheila creates and directs training for this fine company.

Anne Bradley, CRS, GRI, sales associate, John L. Scott Real Estate, Bellevue, Washington. Anne, a top salesperson, created fast and long-term real estate career success by organizing her business professionally, and by creating exceptional customer service.

Julie Davis, CRB, GRI, president, Julie Davis, Inc., REALTORS®, Springfield, Illinois. Julie is a past president of the RB Council and a trailblazer for new real estate ideas.

Amy Dedoyard, associate broker, Windermere Real Estate, Kirkland, Washington. Amy's kudos include various rewards for sales and training.

Laura Duggan, CRB, CRS, president, West Austin Properties, Austin, Texas. Laura applies the newest technology and sales methods to support her active office.

Rick Franz, sales associate, Windermere Real Estate, Bellevue, Washington. Rick rocketed to top real estate success by adapting customer service concepts from the hotel business to real estate sales.

Chris Heagerty, CRB, GRI, president, The Heagerty Company, REALTORS®, Austin, Texas. Chris is a leader in her state CRB chapter and an innovative owner.

Lee Henderson, vice president, innovative trainer, managing partner, Contempo Realty, Inc., Saratoga, California.

Jim McGuffin, GRI, sales associate, Windermere Real Estate, Spokane, Washington. Jim is a top-producing agent in eastern Washington.

Karen McKnight, CRS, GRI, sales associate, Windermere Real Estate, Bellevue, Washington. Karen shares her top-producer sales strategies as an instructor for her company.

Heidi Medina, sales manager, Windermere Real Estate, Edmonds, Washington. Heidi has helped build her office into one of the finest in the Northwest.

Nada Sundermeyer, CRS, GRI, sales associate, John L. Scott Real Estate, Bellevue, Washington. Nada's sales career is one of the highest producing in the nation.

Put the contributions of all these memorable people into your career plan. Add your own interpretation to the principles here. Create the kind of real estate career—and life—you want.

Best wishes,
Carla Cross, CRB

Contents

Figures for Self-Analysis and Planning for Success

Here is a list of some of the self-analysis tools in this book. I chose to list these figures in a group because they are particularly useful in assessing where your business is now—and where you intend for it to go. *A note to managers:* Use these analysis tools to help your experienced agents get back on track.

Surveys

Here are the surveys that I sent to exceptional agents and managers to get their expert opinions for this book. There are two different surveys: one sent to agents and one sent to managers. The striking fact about these responses was how similar and consistent they were, which I've noted throughout the book.

This survey was sent to top-producing agents:

1. From your observations, what is the biggest reason agents fail in their first year?

2. As an agent during your first year, what did you do differently to ensure your success?

3. In your opinion, why do experienced agents (over one year in the business) experience an up-and-down business (leading them to slumps)?

4. How do you avoid the peaks and valleys that so many agents experience?

5. What specifically do you use to keep your attitude up when your business is less than you want it to be?

6. What specific behaviors and/or programs would you recommend to agents who want to change their business from ho-hum to dynamic?

7. In what ways do you see agents spending money unwisely?

8. What are your recommendations for the best use of an agent's promotional budget?

9. How do managers unwittingly hinder an agent's business?

10. What specifically can a manager do to assist an agent who wants to take his or her business to the next higher level?

11. Overall, what advice would you give to an agent who wants to get his or her business back on track?

This survey was sent to top-producing managers:

1. From your observations, what is the biggest reason agents fail in their first year?

2. As an agent during your first year, what did you do differently to ensure your success?

3. In your opinion, why do experienced agents (over one year in the business) experience an up-and-down business (leading them to slumps)?

4. What are some of the ways your successful agents avoid the peaks and valleys that so many agents experience?

5. What specific behaviors and/or programs would you recommend to agents who want to change their business from ho-hum to dynamic?

6. In what ways do you see agents spending money unwisely?

7. What are your recommendations for the best use of an agent's promotional budget?

8. How do some managers unwittingly hinder an agent's business?

9. What specifically do you as a manager do to assist an agent who wants to take his or her business to the next higher level?

10. What assistance (from company, trainers, programs, etc.) would enable you, as a manager, to more effectively help agents gain higher productivity—fast?

11. Overall, what advice would you give to an agent who wants to get his or her business back on track?

1

Finding a Roadmap to Your Future Real Estate Success

When agents are off track, I always make two suggestions: I ask them to make a list of all the reasons why they got into the business and what they love about it. I also tell them to make a list of why they don't want a nine-to-five job. This is a great wake-up call. Second, I tell them to pretend each day is their first day on the job. Once they get back in the mode they started in and became successful, things begin to fall in place!

**—Amy Dedoyard, associate broker,
Kirkland, Washington**

This program is all about getting you from where you are now to greater success. Then, the success itself becomes self-motivating. The greatest motivator to sell a house is to sell a house. Of course. And, it's not just the selling of the house that motivates you. It's all the wonderful accolades that come your way when you do a great job—at anything.

This program is not about the kind of motivation inspired by success breeding success. That's easy. This program is about *how to get to the point* where success starts breeding success. To reach that success-motivating-success cycle requires hard work. I call it *personally driven motivation*—a person is so tough, so committed, so tenacious that he or she can carve out successes in the midst of failures. That's great. That's the ability to hold your dream of real estate success in the midst of *lack of success*. Analyzing exactly how you're creating your business today for the results you're getting and setting in motion a program you know will bring you the rewards you want—that's the reason for this program and this book.

Much of this book is dedicated to helping you through self-analysis. Throughout, you'll see quotes from very successful agents, managers, and owners. I asked 15 pros from around the United States to give me their observations on why agents succeed, why they fail, and how managers can assist success. I'm passing on the invaluable tips these experts included in their surveys, tips that can change your results for the better. The questions from my survey are in the beginning of this book; the list of contributors is in the Acknowledgments. These quoted observations form another part of the ideal roadmap you're putting together. So that you can hear examples of dialogue and sales approaches, I've included two audiotapes in the book-tape package. If you purchase *On Track to Success in 30 Days* as a complete package, the audiotapes are included. However, if you purchase this book in a bookstore, the audiotapes are not included. You can purchase the audiotapes separately by contacting the author at 800-296-2599.

Keep Your "Ideal" Stronger Than Your "Real"

Holding onto your objectives in the face of failure, while you find another method of attaining your goals, is a true measure of character. It's like the basketball guard who, surrounded by three competing players, appears to be boxed in with no way to make a basket. Suddenly, he sights a teammate, unguarded, and deftly passes the ball for an easy bucket. Like that basketball pro, you believe you have the ability to see other ways to your goal, or you wouldn't have started this program.

In this chapter, you'll be able to take the first step toward your success—an analysis of your business from various perspectives. The first look will be at the big picture. You'll compare your vision of what you thought your career would be like with what it is today. You'll investigate how you got that early picture, and what to do about it to ensure different results. I'll help you bring your business back into focus, and, armed with that information, you'll be refreshed and remotivated in your quest for a successful career.

Develop Your Roadmap

In my two decades of real estate practice, I've been asked to help thousands of agents who were dissatisfied with their career results. I've found a major problem is that the agents don't know exactly what's wrong with their careers. Their careers are not bringing the expected income. With this recognition, many agents then make the same mistake. They jump from a feeling of dissatisfaction with their career to immediate and ever-changing conclusions. They run from seminar to seminar, getting more information. Then, they try a little of this, a little of that, running themselves around in circles—with no appreciable results. You don't want to get into this circular syndrome! The first step in creating real estate success is to find out how you're creating the business you have today, or developing a clear roadmap. Then, compare your present roadmap to a roadmap for success.

To get insights into your behavior, let's develop two personal roadmaps:

1. Where you've been, and how you got there
2. Where you want to go, and how to get there

When appropriate, we'll use standardized roadmaps, those behaviors of successful agents that show us an ideal—something to shoot for. When you can see, hear, and feel success, you can replicate it in your own style for greater results.

Roadmap #1: Your Career Vision

Often, an agent's later difficulties stem from perceptions of what he or she thought the business would be like—before coming into the business. Let's start with your vision of your real estate career. Complete the analysis in Figure 1.1, so you can remember your early impressions and expectations before you started selling. These impressions formed your roadmap of the business prior to your *real* experience.

Experiences are different than expectations. In consulting with many agents who've been in the business less than one year, I've found they say that the business is different than they thought it would be. Here are some of the comments agents make after they've been in the business a few months:

-   "I didn't know I'd have to make sales calls. I heard about prospecting, but I thought I'd do it only if business didn't come to me some other way."

Figure 1.1 Your Vision of Your Real Estate Career Prior to Beginning Your Career

What activities did you think were most important to your success?

Where did you think agents spent most of their time?

What activities did you think you'd most enjoy doing?

What activities did you believe you wouldn't enjoy?

What activities did you think would be challenging?

What, if any, challenges did you think you'd face finding clients?

What, if any, challenges, did you think you'd face, working with clients?

What challenges did you think you'd face working with agents inside and outside your office?

Why did you think agents failed? Did you consider failure as a possibility?

What did you think your office and manager would do to assure your success?

How much responsibility did you think your company, office, and manager had for your success?

How much did you expect your training school to provide to assure your success?

What values did you believe were most important to you to "live out" as you started your career?

What did you believe was most important, the knowledge required to "reduce your legal risk" or sales communication skills?

How did you see yourself in sales situations?

What did you think you had as skills that you found you needed later to develop more fully?

- "I didn't think it would take so much time to get a sale. I thought people I would meet would be ready to buy."
- "I thought would-be buyers would be eager to work with me. I was surprised at how distrustful they were, and how difficult it has been to get them to work with me."
- "Buyers are liars. They say they'll work with me and then they buy from somebody else. They're not trustworthy."
- "I didn't think it would be so hard to convince sellers to list at the right price. They don't seem to believe me."
- "Why is it so hard to get buyers and sellers to trust me? I'm credible."
- "I thought my company (or manager) would train me. They said they would. But, the 'training' isn't really helpful or extensive. I thought they'd spend lots of time with me showing me exactly how to answer floor calls, go with me to open houses—really help me get good at this business. What they call 'training' is just a class where we listened to someone."
- "I thought I'd get lots of leads from floor time and open houses."
- "I thought my manager would spend lots of time each day helping me get started."

Differences in idea versus reality create contrasts and conflicts. Let's say you have four gallons of gasoline in your car, and you think you can reach your destination. But, as you travel, you find you must follow a detour. That detour uses up most of your gasoline. Your roadmap has changed, and, with it, your plans for achieving your destination must change. It's the same in real estate. What's different about the business than you thought?

Ask yourself, "What about the gap between my expectations and my experiences is helping me create the *kind* of business I have now?" For example, perhaps you thought (or were told) that because you knew lots of people, you'd do well in real estate. Mark L., in my office, seemed to know half the people in our area! He had worked with them and socialized with them. Both Mark and I thought that, with his contacts, he'd do very well in real estate. Like many managers, I assumed Mark realized he'd have to go tell all these acquaintances that he was now in real estate—and ask for "leads." Bad assumption. Mark had never been in sales. Mark had been a banker. At that time, bankers sat and waited for people to come to them. Mark's view of real estate was like that of banking. You were hired by a bank; the bank opened its doors, and people flocked in for the privilege of doing business with you. The problem was that, even though Mark had lots of acquaintances, Mark never *did* anything with those contacts. He never mailed to them; he never talked to them about real estate opportunities. To them, he was a "secret agent." Because he assumed they would find out he was the best real estate agent in our area (how, mental telepathy?), Mark waited to be "discovered." As with most starlets, he never became a star. It's hard work getting discovered, and 99.9 percent of success, even according to "overnight discoveries," is up to us. We must go out and introduce ourselves to all those we want to meet. That's the only way they're going to discover us!

We have beliefs and expectations that are different than the actual experiences. Using the material you generated in Figure 1.1, write some of the contrasts you've noticed between what you *thought* the business would be like and what it's like—for you. In your daily schedule, are you still trying to make your pre-real estate vision of what the business is like come true?

Roadmap #2: Develop Your Present Job Description

You've compared and contrasted what you thought real estate was like to what you know it's like now. It's time to develop your present job description. First, write down all the business activities you've completed this past month. Now, using Figure 1.2, tally the number of hours you've spent doing "revenue-producing activities." Tally the number of hours you've spent doing "support activities." Look at your list and time allotments. What does that list tell you that you think is the most important to accomplish in your real estate career? What are you getting good at? Now, create your job description based on how you've prioritized your tasks. That's the roadmap for your career that you've chosen. Contrast that with the vision you had of yourself as a real estate agent prior to your career start. What's similar? What's different? As we continue your self-analysis in these chapters, we'll be developing specific plans of action to change your beliefs and habits to assure that you create a job description for success—and are able to follow it.

Industry-provided job descriptions mislead agents. As a national speaker, I meet thousands of agents and managers each year. Managers frequently give me their materials to review. In one of these "encounters," I got an agent's job description (Figure 1.3). This figure was created by a management consultant. Reading it, what do you think this manager thinks are priorities for a real estate agent? Looks to me like the manager thinks "support time" activities are priorities, not "revenue-producing activities" (prospecting, showing, closing). My experience in working

Figure 1.2 Analysis: Time and Activities

The activities:

Hours spent
this month

Revenue-producing activities:

Proactive prospecting (you go out and find
potential clients/customers) _____

Reactive prospecting (open houses/floor time) _____

Qualifying/counseling buyers _____

Showing buyers homes _____

Closing buyers/negotiating offers _____

Giving marketing presentations to sellers/
qualifying sellers _____

Listing marketable properties _____

Attending purchase and sale presentations
on behalf of your sellers _____

Total hours: _____

Supportive activities:

Attending meetings _____

Paperwork/follow-up _____

Previewing properties _____

Other: _____

Total hours: _____

Analysis:

What you consider most important, according to the time and effort you're expending:

Your job description now:

Conclusions:

with managers is that this consultant thinks like lots of other managers. We managers like to organize the office, not tend to the individual's development. So, we schedule activities that are easy for us to organize at an "office" level (organizing all agents at once). These include meetings, floor time, office tours, and open houses. A manager can schedule these at an office level and easily observe whether the agents meet their "obligations." However, there's one problem. These activities don't bring direct sales results. Why? They're not revenue-producing (with the exception of floor time and open houses). Unwittingly, through their scheduling and procedures to assure their office runs smoothly, managers frequently provide agents a job description for a low producer! The agent, wanting to "fit in," follows this scheduling and experiences low production.

Successful agents spend their time prospecting.　Successful agents spend more time by far, than unsuccessful agents, finding prospects (proactively), presenting, and closing buyers and sellers. A job description for a *successful* real estate agent, then, would put these activities as priorities. But, for managers, there's one problem in supporting this kind of job description: The revenue-producing, critical-to-success activities aren't easy to schedule, manage, and monitor for individuals. In fact, they can't be scheduled, managed, and monitored at the *office* level. They must be managed at the individual's level. This requires much more dedication and tenacity by the manager. However, if these are the activities critical to the agent's success, it makes sense that we managers would want to switch to managing these activities, right? In fact, though, to switch to managing these activities, managers must accept that our job is to *help individual agents create successful businesses.* Laura Duggan, CRB, owner of West Austin Properties, Austin, Texas, sees managers who by managing the old way, through controlling office scheduling, thwart agents' success:

- "Managers unwittingly hinder an agent's business by not giving them individual support and attention through coaching and mentoring."

Good systems for managing activities exist.　Managing to these individually completed activities is very difficult without a system. That's why I use *Up & Running in 30 Days* (Carla Cross, Real Estate Education Company, Inc.® 1995) with all my new agents. With it, I can guide new agents in learning how to create a system for success, while teaching them self-management. Even with this system, I need additional support, because my management responsibilities are too various

Figure 1.3   Example of Job Description for a Licensed Real Estate Agent (*not* Carla's version)

1. Establish—with your manager's help—your professional (sales) goals for the running year, including monthly, weekly, and daily goals, and set up how to achieve them.

2. Know the company's marketing area—its geography, demographics, socioeconomic factors, neighborhood characteristics, schools, stores, transportation and recreation facilities.

3. Know the inventory (of residential properties for sale). Be thoroughly familiar with the listings of this office. Know the company's listings. Be familiar with the listings of our multiple listing service.

4. Hold floor time (or "Up Time") or equivalent. Serve regularly scheduled periods in the office to: (a) answer incoming phone calls; (b) serve walk-in customers; (c) take messages for out of office agents.

5. Get listings. Fill out exclusive listing agreement; get it signed by seller.

6. Show and sell property. Earnest money properly completed, signed, submitted to seller, and accepted and signed by seller.

7. Go on tours ("caravans").

8. Attend all scheduled meetings.

9. Follow up on all transactions (paperwork, phone calls, etc.).

10. Appraise property.

11. Maintain all forms, sales tools, etc.

12. Meet "continuing education" (clock hour) requirements and maintain professional development.

13. Favorably represent the company.
    (a) Maintain personal appearance compatible with your market and reflecting favorably the image of the company.
    (b) Maintain your car/a car. Maintain in safe, clean, and comfortable condition a car of such type, make, and class as to reflect favorably on the company and the agent.

14. Maintain a steady flow of prospective clients/customers through referrals, prospecting, etc.

15. Know (and follow) office procedures:
    (a) Timing and flow of paperwork
    (b) Approvals required
    (c) Distribution of materials, information
    (d) Hours and schedules
    (e) Communication requirements
    (f) Telephone and message procedures
    (g) Operation of office equipment

There may be more job functions specific to your own office or your company. If there are, be sure to include them here.

to devote the "think" time needed to assure the new agent gets started right—and fast. So, in addition, I employ a coach for each new agent.

"But, I want to do it *my way*."   Most new agents come into the business with a different vision of the business than they find as reality. Whose responsibility is it to help prospective agents get the right vision? The manager's. That doesn't mean, though, that we can force agents to accept the right job description! I insist each prospective agent read the *Career* book and review *Up & Running in 30 Days* and *CrossCoaching* prior to affiliation. All new agents with us sign a contract stating they understand and agree to do the work, and agree to have their activities managed during the coaching period. Still, some agents try to "do it their way"—and fail. At that point, my experience as a manager tells me to help that agent make a career change!

Here is a job description for a successful agent.   When teaching managers, I've found very few have created a job description for the successful real estate agent. In fact, before I started teaching the CRB management courses, *I* didn't have an agent's job description either to show prospective agents. Here's the job description I created (Figure 1.4). Note that it has the sales-oriented activities listed first, in the order that they must occur to get results. Then, the supportive activities are listed in a separate section. How does it differ from your job description?

New agents' expectations generally are unrealized.   We've investigated what you thought the job would be, what you think your job is now, and a job description for success. Besides guessing about *what* you'd be doing before you started your career, you had some expectations about the amount of money you'd make in your first year, and how fast you'd start making that money. If you're like many agents, those expectations weren't realized. According to the survey I completed before writing my first book, most new agents have much higher expectations for success in their first year than they experience. The largest group in my survey expected *first-year incomes* of $40,000 to $70,000. In contrast, according to the National Association of REAL-TORS®, the average REALTOR® makes about $24,000 a year (for *all* REALTORS® in the business, no matter how long). In addition, according to my survey, these new agents expected success *fast*. The largest group expected to make a sale their first 30 days in the business. Although I can't find statistics on the early success rates of first-year agents, my casual observation of agents in my area is that most new agents make very little money their first year, and few agents make one sale even in their first *three* months.

Figure 1.4 A Job Description of a Successful Real Estate Agent

There are two categories of activities real estate agents complete:

1. *Business Development* (prospecting, showing, selling)
2. *Business Support* (all other activities)

A successful real estate agent completes these categories of activities with these priorities:

1. *Business Development* Activities First

   A. *Prospect:* Find potential customers and clients by identifying and calling on best target markets, consistently and frequently.

   B. *Show and list:* Sales activities generated as a result of prospecting activities
      Showing homes to *qualified* customers
      Listing *marketable, qualified* properties (those that will sell in normal market time)

   C. *Sell:* The only two activities that assure a paycheck
      1. Sell a home
      2. Your listing sells

All other activities are supportive to the activities above the line, and should be completed only enough to support the sales activities required to get a commission check.

2. Business Support

   Includes all activities that are not "sales" activities, such as:

      Preview properties/tours
      Do paperwork/sales follow-up
      Education
      Meetings
      Return telephone calls

Reprinted with permission from *The Recruiter* by Carla Cross, Carla Cross Seminars, 1993.

The realities of new agents' first year results don't match their prelicense visions. When reality sets in, most new agents get discouraged and give up. Here are some comments from my survey of exceptional managers and agents, observing why agents fail in their first year:

- From Laura Duggan, CRS, CRB, owner: "They quit too soon; do not have enough financial support to begin and sustain their business."

- From Nada Sundermeyer, CRS, GRI, sales associate: "They fail to work on dollar-productivity behavior (prospecting)."

- From Karen McKnight, CRS, GRI, sales associate: "They don't have enough self-discipline and persistence. They think real estate is an easy business. They don't understand a key concept in real estate: We not only have to prospect for customers, we prospect for inventory."

- From Julie Davis, CRB, owner: "They fail to prospect. They fail to understand that prospecting is the most important part of their job and the only thing that their manager won't do for them."

These exceptional agents and owners quoted above have observed patterns of failure by watching thousands of new agents. Although this is an unhappy subject, it's important for us to recognize. If we don't know what we're doing wrong, how can we correct it? I quote these people here so that you can get insights into your business patterns. Are there similarities between your self-analysis of your business patterns (your roadmap), and the behaviors these pros are observing?

Build a prototype schedule. You've compared your job description with the description of a successful agent. You've analyzed your use of time. Here are two figures that can further help you get a new roadmap for your real estate business. The first, Figure 1.5, is a prototype schedule to help you reallocate your time. The second, Figure 1.6, is an allocation of time for certain activities in your weekly scheduling. If your time allotment from your earlier analysis looked very different, you may be discouraged at this point. There's good news, though. You have a track record to compare. You know how challenging time management is. Although I teach this "activity prioritization" concept to new agents, they tend to "nod" through it. They don't realize that they will be pushed and pulled in so many directions. Didn't you find this one of your greatest challenges as a newer agent? You had that wonderful prelicense job description. Then, reality struck. What you ended up with was a job description developed through crisis management. Most of us have to go through that cycle to get back on track.

Figure 1.5 Prototype Schedule

TIME COMMITMENTS: How to allocate your time to assure quick success.

ACTIVITY	DAILY	NO./WEEK	HOURS
Business Developing Plan:*	4 hours	5 days	20
Open House		once a week	3 – 4
Floor Time		1 day	3
Business Meeting	1 hour	once a week	1
Office Education	1 hour	1 day	1
Mgr/Agent Counseling		once a week	1 – 2
Previewing	2 hours	5 days	10

SCHEDULE

MON:
8:00 – 8:45 Meet with Manager / Paperwork / Calls
8:45 – 9:30 Business Meeting
9:30 – 12:30 New Office Listing Tour
LUNCH
1:30 – 5:30 Business Plan

TUES: Day off .... TAKE IT !!!

WED:
8:00 – 9:00 Paperwork
9:00 – 10:00 Business Plan
10:00 – 12:00 Inspect
1:00 – 5:00 Business Plan

THURS:
8:00 – 9:00 Paperwork
9:00 – 11:00 Inspect
12:00 – 3:00 Floor Time / Buyer Tour
3:00 – 6:00 Business Plan

FRI:
8:00 – 8:45 Paperwork
8:45 – 9:15 Office Class
9:30 – 12:00 Inspect
1:00 – 5:00 Business Plan
7:00 – 8:00 Listing Presentation

SAT:
9:00 – 12:00 Business Plan
1:00 – 4:00 Listing Presentation / Buyer Tour
4:00 – 5:00 Paperwork

SUN:
12:00 – 2:00 Business Plan
2:00 – 5:00 Open House or Buyer Tour
5:00 – 6:00 Listing Presentation

*Your plan for finding and working with buyers and sellers. See the four-week plan in this book. It's a good business developing plan.

Figure 1.6 A Regenerative Plan for Higher Income

	Hours	Blocks	When
1. Schedule revenue-producing activities first:			
Prospecting*	20	1-2 hrs.	People are home
Appointments to show/list	5	1 hr.	People are home
(Purchase presentations/negotiations)	?	2 hrs.	
2. Schedule support activities second:			
Office meeting	1	1	
Office tour	3	3	
Preview properties	6	2 hrs.	Convenient for you—for listing, showing
Paperwork	5	1/2 hr.	Early in morning Late afternoon
Lunch	5	1 hr.	

*As you find qualified buyers and sellers, you'll be using some of your prospecting hours to work with them. As a result of this work, you'll be doing purchase presentations and negotiating. You'll need to make adjustments in your time allotments. Remember to keep prospecting and showing while you're selling, or you'll find yourself in a "slump."

At the beginning of this chapter, I talked about the somewhat circuitous routes we take to get to our goals. These aren't really circuitous, if we use them to our long-term benefit. They're really critical to help us recognize the lessons we're trying to teach ourselves. Analysis and redirection are part of our development, part of our path to success. You're lucky. You've had enough experience in real estate to have a track record to compare. It's not what you did. It's what you do now with it.

Summary

In this chapter, we've developed a prelicense roadmap, what you remembered you thought the business was like. Then, we developed your present job description. Finally, we compared it to the job description of a successful real estate agent. You've gotten some insights into how you got to where you are and some insights into how to get from where you are to success. As we continue our analysis, I'll be providing dozens of tips specifically on how you can redirect your career—to get on track to success.

Your Tune-Up for Chapter 1

✓ Complete the analysis in Figure 1.1.

✓ Complete the analysis in Figure 1.2. Compare it to the prototype time allotments in Figure 1.6. Write down the discrepancies. Decide on five adjustments you'll make in your scheduling for the next month, based on your analysis. Put these adjustments into your daily schedule.

✓ Compare your present job description with the one in Figure 1.4. Analyze the differences. Make three adjustments in your job description to match that of the successful agent.

2

Off Track and Determined to Get Back On

Agents go through growth cycles. Their needs and expectations change from one year to four years and ten years naturally. Agents forget to take the time to really assess where they are and what they want out of their real estate career. They get so busy working they forget to dream. Then, they wake up to find they are involved in something so different from the original dream that they become disillusioned and begin a slow downward spiral. It is imperative to STOP and dream and replan your business.

—Heidi Medina, sales manager,
Edmonds, Washington

Driving down the street one day, I saw a beat-up old car, with a custom license plate saying "WhrAmI." I thought it was pretty ironic that the owner of that car would spend money on *that* vanity plate. The plate probably cost him more than the car was worth! At least, the owner of the car admitted not really knowing where he or she was. . . .

In this chapter, I'll introduce three analytical concepts to help you discover where you are right now in your career. This is a chapter that will be very meaningful to you if you are not getting the results you want from your career. I'll provide some specific recommendations for you, so that you can make the adjustments to get back on track in those areas where you determined you need information, redirection, and skills.

The Career Life Cycle

The first analytical tool for you to put to use in your business analysis is the "career life cycle" (Figure 2.1). Most of this chapter is devoted to this concept, for it will give you invaluable insights into your career management. This look at an agent's real estate business is taken from the world of marketing. By studying products, marketers observed that, like people, each had a "life." Over the term of the product's life, the marketers identified four pretty distinct stages of development: Introduction, growth, maturity, and decline. They call this concept "product life cycle" and they use it in planning marketing campaigns. During each of these stages of a product's life, marketers apply certain marketing strategies. And, in each of these stages, the strategies must change to prolong the life of the product.

In the first, the products are introduced, to great excitement and anticipation. The developers of the product are excited about the product, and "sold" on the idea that the product is something that the public would embrace as enthusiastically as they did. Lots of time and money are spent on the introduction of the product, including training

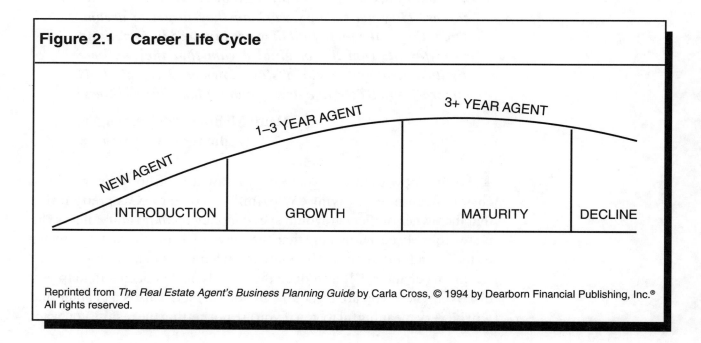

Figure 2.1 Career Life Cycle

NEW AGENT

1–3 YEAR AGENT

3+ YEAR AGENT

| INTRODUCTION | GROWTH | MATURITY | DECLINE |

salespeople and representatives. To succeed, the product must be widely promoted.

Let's relate this to the life cycle of a real estate agent. First, there are the new agents. Isn't their experience very similar to that of a new product? They come into the business highly motivated, thinking that the public will immediately embrace and accept their services. They spends their (or the company's) time and money getting trained. They spend their (or the company's) time and money on introducing themselves to their potential clientele, for no one knows they're in the business. Their manager is excited to have them in the office, and has high expectations for them. As with many new products, new agents are often undercapitalized, and have a short period to "make it or break it."

What Can Go Wrong in the Introduction Phase?

This undercapitalization and short-time expectation can lead to cutting corners, wrong decisions, and using marketing tactics that hurt the product or service over the long term. For example, in the world of products, sometimes the advertisements to introduce the product—to get us to buy it—are misleading. Early on, that type of promotion looks like it's working to get immediate results. However, when customers find out they've been misled, they'll never use the product again. Without return use, products, services, *and* agents fail.

Sometimes a new agent resorts to this expedient approach to get business. Here's what happens. The agent has vowed to keep the customer's best interests in mind. However, all those highfalutin thoughts about "exceptional customer service" may go out the window when the agent *needs* a listing or a sale. So, in an agent's introductory period, an agent can learn bad sales habits because they give him an immediate "success." However, they don't set up a good long-term business. By putting self first and the customer last, the agent has low customer satisfaction levels. Then, angry customers complain, and complaining customers don't send referrals. Finally, the agent has to spend lots of advertising money finding more unsuspecting, new customers, because his or her old customers aren't sources of business.

Bait and switch still happens in real estate.   New agents tell me that they want to get a listing. They think that really means they're "in the business." They tell me that they don't care if it's overpriced, because it's more important to have a listing. They tell me that they'll get sign and ad calls, helping them launch their businesses. They say that they don't care if the home sells. They intend to use that listing as a bait and switch. When they show the home to the customer, the customer will know it's overpriced, and the agent will show other homes that are better-priced. They're using that listing to get customers.

Now, you may be saying, that's not in the client's best interests. (You know what I mean, if you've had your home on the market recently. It's hard work.) Taking overpriced listings is only in the agent's best interest—short-term. However, many agents still use this bait and switch tactic. In our multiple listing area, over 60 percent of the listings are taken that way. Less than 40 percent sell in half a year. (By way of comparison, our average time on the market, for a mid-priced home, is less than 30 days.) As I observe the listing practices of many agents, most of the time, agents are making sales decisions based on their own short-term need—a listing. They do not have the client in mind. We know from National Association of REALTORS® studies that the seller gets much less in proceeds the longer his or her home is on the market. We know that no demand is created, so the seller has to negotiate with a buyer who has the upper hand. We know that leads to a less attractive sale for the seller.

Why, then, if we agents *say* we want to provide excellent customer service, do we take overpriced listings? In my opinion, I think it's because we managers haven't figured out that overpriced listings are the main determinant of our less-than-excellent customer-service ratings. Overpriced listings lead to customer dissatisfaction, which leads to negative gossip about the agent and company, which leads to *less* business in the long-term. In the beginning of the career life cycle, then, it's important that agents and managers start the kind of business practices that lead to a continuation and growth of the business. Delighted clients beget more delighted clients—at a much lower cost than advertising to another group of unsuspecting strangers! (And, we won't be accused of engaging in sales tactics often attributed to used car salespeople!)

Are you in the introduction phase of real estate sales? As we continue through these chapters, we'll be taking a very close look at how you're doing your business. Right now, I'll make some overall recommendations to you if you're in the introduction phase of real estate sales. In general, you're in "introduction" if you've been in the business less than one year. The biggest mistakes agents make in the introduction phase are

- not prospecting enough to generate leads to qualify "tough";
- not spending enough time on the sales path (See Figure 2.2.);
- getting listings to "get listings," destroying their image and wasting their resources, teaching themselves expedient sales methods;

- showing unqualified buyers, then wondering how to close (you can't close if you don't know why they want to buy or if they can't afford to buy);

- looking at the business as short-term (if I don't sell a home in the first month, I'm out of the business).

Agents in their first year need to concentrate on short-term goals (setting goals for prospecting, showing, qualifying). Using a program like the one described in my *Up & Running in 30 Days* gets agents into the right business habits and cycles. The four-week program in this book is similar to the one in *Up & Running in 30 Days*, but it is tailored a bit differently to address the untapped resources of business that experienced agents have available. So that newer agents learn business practices that predict high customer satisfaction levels, newer agents should work with an agency that teaches, supports, and manages by these ideals. Unguided, the newer agent may make assumptions that, because certain business practices seen in the office or in the field are allowed, they are the best business practices to follow. New agents learn to sell mainly by watching how others sell in the office.

For example, John joined our office a few months ago. He had a friend in another office who has been in the real estate business over ten years. John was tempted to follow the listing practices of his friend—list them high and try to "schmooze" the seller down in price, while using the listing to get customers. His friend had asked him to colist a property with him, using the old "list high, keep the seller in the dark, and get leads" approach. John's coach and I asked John how many new buyers he might get from the sign and ad. He thought "three." Then, we asked him if he thought he'd get referrals from the seller. No, he said, not if the listing didn't sell. We asked him how he'd handle the seller's complaints. We asked him when he thought those complaints would start. Agents tell me it's about a month from the time the listing is taken to the time when the seller calls, angry. Finally, we asked him how many referrals he could get from the seller, if the listing sold quickly, for close to full price. He thought "five." We asked him how many leads he could get by going around the neighborhood when the home sold, telling people about his success and asking for leads. He thought "two." After he added the "lead potential," and the "heartache potential," he wanted to list properties properly!

However, he had already committed to his friend for co-listing this home. You guessed it. John suffered through the seller's abuse. The home didn't sell. They lost the listing, and they lost the ability to create other high-quality referrals from a delighted seller. John, by the way, is a terrific listing agent, having seen the results of each type of listing strategy! My advice to you: When in doubt, the newer agent should always check with his manager. The real estate business is changing dramatically. However, many experienced agents are still practicing real estate using manipulative sales techniques.

The Growth Phase of the Life Cycle

After a product is introduced, and some consumers start using it, the marketing gears shift to expansion of the market. Money and resources are plowed back into marketing to help more buyers know about and purchase the product. Generally, the marketing budget is very strong in this phase. In this phase, it's critical that the product has been accepted and has gotten terrific reviews from its first customers. Why? Because, if the product is not strongly accepted, the marketing dollars needed to "get the product over the hump" are too large. In other words, the marketers have to spend too much money to get a return on their investments.

For real estate agents, consumer trust is especially important in the 1990s, and as we head into the twenty-first century. Treating the customer right is the only defense against the customer choosing *no* real estate agent the next time! (Think about the possibilities that the Internet allows potential customers and clients. . . .) The American marketing world has discovered that if the strategy for getting customers costs return business—it's not a good strategy. (Think of how the Japanese auto makers took away our market a few years ago.) Keeping the customers you already have has become more important than getting new ones, especially as you move from the introduction phase of your business to the growth phase. If you don't have a strategy that gets you into the business and propels you toward keeping the customers you've got, you just put yourself into the position of having to be a new agent over and over again.

Are you in the growth phase of your career?   Let's identify the real estate agent's growth phase as approximately one to four years in the business—for now. If you're in the growth phase, you should ask yourself these questions:

- Have I established a large enough old customer base to go back to it to get more business?

- Are my old customers happy enough with my service that I can rely on them to give me testimonials and send me business?

- What about my business practices gets me repeat business and referrals?

- What about my business practices costs me repeat business and referrals?
- Am I conducting my business as a growth phase product business would conduct its business?
- What's identifiable about my business now that I can use to promote my business?

A systematized approach can help you accelerate your career advancement. Let's go to my "panel" of experts for their insights on why agents in this growth period fail to achieve the results they want:

- From Lee Henderson, sales manager: "They find a comfort zone and discontinue prospecting. When their pipeline empties, they experience a 'slump.'"
- From Sheila Bell, CRB, CRS, GRI, trainer: "They have no specific plan for creating continual flow of business."
- From Jim McGuffin, top sales agent: "They don't do enough follow-up on ongoing marketing with friends and past customers."

I just reread all the answers in my survey to the question, "Why do experienced agents (over one year in the business) experience an 'up and down' business?" Overall, the answers had to do with inconsistent prospecting and little adherence to a business plan. If you're in your growth phase, do you have an overall plan for success? When's the last time you looked at it? (The four-week plan in *On Track to Success in 30 Days* will give you new revenue-producing habits to assure that your pipeline doesn't dry up ever again.)

Is it really the introductory or growth phase? In working with thousands of agents, I've found that one of the biggest challenges to the "growth agent" is to determine whether he or she *truly* is in the growth phase. Just because you've been in the business over a year doesn't mean you're ready to go into the growth phase. Agents who are truly in this phase can shift from generating new business leads to generating leads from old business. (This is every agent's dream.) If you're truly in the growth phase, you should be getting half your leads from old customers and clients. However, to build your business with half your leads coming from past customers and clients, you must have

- a customer-client base of at least 100, and
- a customer-client base of thrilled, delighted people.

If you don't have this kind of customer base to rely on, you're not in the growth phase. You must go back to the introductory phase and do the kinds of prospecting activities that new agents do to create business. The good news is that you don't have to learn your way around the office or your multiple listing service, as you did when you were really "new."

The Maturity Phase of the Product Life Cycle—and Afterward

We watch some "seasoned" agents, and we think, boy, what would we give to be in that position. They have a stable business that seems to almost run itself. It looks as though it could go on that way forever. Well, in a minute, I'm going to destroy all of those illusions!

Let's first clarify exactly what the "maturity" phase is. After the product is introduced, and, hopefully, grows, it settles into the "mature" phase. Naive product producers think they've "got it made." Like some adults in life who think the world should be blessed by their mere presence (not their work), product producers in the "mature" phase think that the world owes them the courtesy of buying the product. This complacency with the status quo is lethal. In fact, it leads to the inevitable last phase, the "decline."

There are ways, though, to avoid slipping into decline. In the product life cycle, a good example would be the Taurus automobile. For several years, the Taurus had the same body style. It had been the bestselling car in the United States—in its growth phase. But, as the public saw every third person drive a Taurus, the Taurus started to get "boring." Its market share slipped. It was *declining* in popularity. The frightening thing about the mature phase of a product or career life cycle is that it doesn't stay stable and merely level off. When a product or career reaches maturity, unfortunately, it's naturally headed downward into the last phase—decline. To stop this natural decline, product producers must take strong, clear actions against what's *natural* (kind of like those Hollywood stars getting face-lifts). So, what did Taurus producers do? They stopped the inevitable decline by pushing Taurus back into the "growth" phase. How? By introducing a new, revolutionary body style. In order to revitalize the automobile, they couldn't merely put some gee-gaws inside or paint the exterior a new color. They had to completely retool the automobile—just like smart companies are retooling themselves to compete in the twenty-first century. Along with that retooling came an aggressive, growth-oriented, fresh advertising campaign to persuade the public that the Taurus was again "cutting edge."

The dangers of thinking you've got it made in the mature career phase.   If you've been in the business for over seven or eight years, chances are you're acting like a mature agent. You're getting most of your leads from repeat business and referrals. You've built up a strong enough business that you do most of your business based on prebuilt trust and confidence. What's wrong with that? Nothing, so far. But a self-defeating pattern can develop with the agent who's getting most of his business on repeat and referrals.

Here's what I mean. Our mature agent, Martha, is referred to George and Betty Smith, who want to sell their home. George and Betty also were referred to John Schlock, of ABC Realty. Now, Martha knows John Schlock, and she thinks his last name is appropriate. Of course, though, she can't say this to sellers George and Betty. Martha's in kind of a bind here. She relies on word-of-mouth for her business, and she relies on this word-of-mouth to build her credibility to the point where she has no need to build it herself. This works fine when she's not competing with another agent, and the sellers already think she's the best thing since sliced bread. It doesn't work so well when she's competing. You see, she has no testimonials in writing, no Professional Portfolio (personal marketing), no visual marketing presentation, no statistics systematized to teach George and Betty the principles of good real estate marketing. Why not? Because she works with those who refer business to her, Martha doesn't need these credibility-builders very often, as those newer agents do. And, when she does, it's too late to create them. This mature business approach can result in lost listings or overpriced listings. This makes Martha mad, but to do anything about it Martha would have to admit she needs to quit acting like a mature agent and push herself back into the growth phase. Just like Taurus, she needs to "retool" herself. You, dear reader, may be like Martha. Congratulations on taking the risk to even look at your business today. Many Marthas in real estate are unwittingly waiting out the inevitable—their descent into decline.

What you should be aware of if you're in the mature career phase.   With real estate practice changing so dramatically and so fast for companies, offices, managers, and agents, this mature phase is the most dangerous. The danger of lulling ourselves into complacency in our mature phase is that, without our knowing it, we've slipped into decline. So, to find out if you're in the mature phase, ask yourself:

- Am I relying almost solely on old customers and clients to send me referrals?

- Am I relying almost solely on my reputation to list properties at the right price?

- Am I losing listings, or pricing them too high, when I don't have strong enough credibility with sellers?

- Am I resisting putting my credibility statements in writing (and/or my marketing program) because I rarely need to establish my credibility?

- Have I introduced a new business practice into my business in the last two years?

- Have I looked at my business as though I were a new agent—in the last two years?

- What's my attitude about technology? Am I waiting for it to go away?

The Decline Phase of the Life Cycle

As you can imagine, a product can travel through the product life cycle in years—or months. Usually it takes a few years to go through the cycle. Let's take the example of the Yugo, the Yugoslavian automobile that was introduced to the American public in 1985. Money and energy were spent on its introduction. It never gathered the impetus to get into the growth phase with vigor. Unfortunately, it had poor quality and, thus, poor customer acceptance. Then, there was no testimonial energy that was available to marketers to take it to growth quickly. It quickly slipped from growth, to maturity, to decline—all within a decade. Now, Yugos are having somewhat of a resurrection—not as cars, but as pop art. They're being made into everything from accordions to confessionals. If you were a marketer, what would you have done to Yugo to resuscitate it when it was in decline? If you answered 'nothing', you're right. It was too late. When a product or service starts its descent from the peak of maturity toward decline, it's pretty much over. The lesson from the business world to agents in the mature phase is this:

> *To avoid slipping from the peak of maturity to decline, we must reinvent ourselves as though we were in the beginning of the growth period. If we don't, someone else will take our market share.*

Microsoft's Bill Gates said it well in stating that their company's objective was to *replace its products itself before the public perceived they needed replacing, and before the competitors came up with a replacement.* No resting on the laurels.

How to tell if you're in decline. Frequently, agents who've been in the business for decades are actually in decline. This decline can be identified several ways:

- The agent's production diminishes, even though he or she seems to be working.
- The agent doesn't keep in contact with past customers and clients.
- The agent seems uninterested in what's going on in the office.
- The agent, when introduced to a new marketing tool, says, "It won't work for me in my market."
- The agent resents the success of newer agents.
- The agent is resistant to market trends and industry changes.
- The agent expends energy dampening the dreams, strategies, and ideas of the introductory or growth agent.

What to do if you're in decline.   Just like a product, when an agent is in decline, there is no going back. After reading this book, completing the assignments, and doing the four-week plan, you'll know if you're in decline. At that point, do yourself a favor and investigate alternatives to real estate commissioned sales (such as property management or appraisal). The industry will continue changing more rapidly, and decliners expend energy trying to turn back the clock. Help the industry by supporting the enthusiasm, acceptance, and motivations of those in the introduction and growth phases of the business. Your leaving the business unleashes this energy, and frees your energy for the pursuits still in your heart to accomplish.

Your Attitude About Sales

In this section, we've explored the analytical tool, the 'career life cycle'. There's a second big picture concept we should investigate here. That's your attitude toward sales. I've interviewed hundreds of prospective agents in my two decades in the business. It's amazing to me how many times they tell me they don't want sales on their business cards. They don't think much of salespeople! So, they're going to become salespeople? They've already doomed themselves at the start. They don't want to sell. Then, when sales skill courses are recommended, they reject them. They either think they don't need to sell, they don't want to sell—or they think there's nothing to "selling." To evaluate your attitude about sales, take a blank sheet of paper and write all the thoughts that occur to you about "sales." How do you see yourself as a salesperson? Do you have attitudes about sales that may be inhibiting your career?

Success Is Getting on the Sales Path with Skill

Figure 2.2 shows you another big-picture idea. It's a simple, yet powerful concept, the Sales Path. When you're on the path, you're on the way to sales revenue. When you're doing any other activities, you're not *selling* real estate. It's most important to get on the path. Then, you'll make more money on the path as you develop sales skill. Which is your favorite part of the path? Which part of the path do you avoid? When's the last time you worked at developing sales skill on the

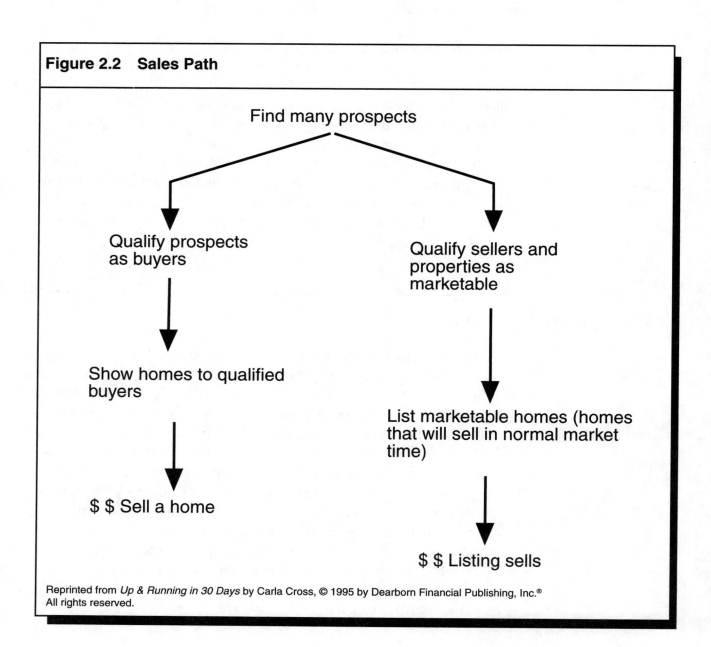

Figure 2.2   Sales Path

Find many prospects

Qualify prospects as buyers

Qualify sellers and properties as marketable

Show homes to qualified buyers

List marketable homes (homes that will sell in normal market time)

$ $ Sell a home

$ $ Listing sells

path? How many hours per week to you spend in class, listening to tapes, reading, and practicing to improve your sales skills? How important do you believe improving your sales skills to be? The four-week plan in this program will lay out a simple, effective sales path plan. In addition, on the audiotapes, I'll be role playing some sales skills for you.

Summary

In this chapter, we've explored three big-picture sales analysis concepts. The first was the concept of life cycles. Although this concept originated in the world of marketing, it's directly applicable to an agent's career. Understanding where each of us is in the career life cycle is vital if we are to make the career moves toward greater success. The success of a product depends on its marketing strategies throughout its life cycle. Most important, the success of a product today depends on its avoiding the downside of maturity, decline, and retooling itself to stay in the vibrant growth stage. It's the same with your career. Your success as an agent depends on your managing your career at each stage. Getting yourself on track requires that you recognize your career stage and decide where you want your career to be in the career life cycle. Then, you can take the steps needed to retool your career for success into the twenty-first century.

The second big-picture idea introduced in this chapter is your attitude about "sales." Feeling good about what you're doing is key to creating more career success.

Finally, the third concept in this chapter was the Sales Path. With this tool, you can ask yourself how much effort you are expending in each step of the sales path and how skilled you are at each of the steps on this path. You can review the amount of time and energy you've been spending in increasing your sales skills. Now, as we continue this program, you'll be making an individualized plan for greater success through tackling those areas you feel need attention.

Your Tune-Up for Chapter 2

✓ This week, interview three successful sales agents in your desired career phase. Apply one strategy you learn from each to your business.

✓ Decide on five changes in your business, based on your analysis of your career phase and your desired career phase. Start those changes this week.

✓ Read two sales books a week for the next four weeks. In each book, apply one sales skill each week for new sales repertoire.

✓ Listen to sales audiotapes 20 minutes per day, five days per week for the next month. Weekly, apply one new sales skill you learn, until the sales skill is natural for you.

3

Steering Clear: Managing Your Attitude

> *I keep my attitude "up" with the certain knowledge that I have control of the situation. I know that if I make calls and contacts and concentrate on the positives, the business will come. That knowledge comes from experience. By consistently working my sphere, my business tends not to be market sensitive.*
>
> **—Anne Bradley, sales associate, Bellevue, Washington**

What surprised me as I began this chapter were the virtual bombardment of ideas. Evidently, my subconscious must have lots of opinions about the subject, "Managing Your Attitude." I know keeping a positive outlook is a very important component for real estate success. Yet, I've found that very few of the agents who go into real estate have the ready-made mental toughness to withstand the disappointments and rejections of the business. Sometimes they fail simply because they let their attitude manage them! It seems to me that most agents (and we managers) could benefit from some additional skills in learning to manage attitude. I think this skill can be learned. So, in this chapter I'm going to give you methods of organizing your thoughts so that they support your roadmap for success. You'll be able to recognize when your attitudes sometimes orders *you* around. You'll get strategies to get control of your attitude—and order *it* around—to create greater success.

Part of an Agent's Job Description

Managing your attitude is part of your job. In interviewing hundreds of agents after they've been in real estate several months, most of them tell me that they didn't know real estate would be so personally challenging. They didn't know how easy it was to get "down" or how quickly they could lose that excitement, that enthusiasm they felt as new agents. Think back to when you were a new agent. How long did that initial excitement, enthusiasm, and hope last?

According to my survey of agents new to real estate, they expected to make a sale their first 30 days in the business. Most of them didn't accomplish that. So, if their expectations weren't met, they lost that enthusiasm. Most agents tell me it only took them about a month to start questioning themselves about whether they should be in this business. Because they didn't realize they'd have so many ups and downs, they weren't prepared to deal with the downs. Unfortunately, then, they talked themselves out of the business—and didn't even know they were doing it! Knowing and applying what's in this chapter, then, can make the difference between success and failure in your career.

Who's Responsible for Your Success?

"They're just lucky." "They get things handed to them." "A buyer walked into his open house and bought from him—that's the only way he got a sale." "The manager gives her all the leads." Many of us spend too much of our time comparing ourselves to others. We find all kinds of reasons why the other person is doing better than we are. Okay. Let's say all the statements above are true. So what? What does it mean to you? If you conclude from your comparisons to others that the deck is stacked for their success, not yours, you're right. You've just let situations take you out of control of your own destiny.

For example, George, in my office, was having trouble being assertive enough with sellers. So, they were taking advantage of his service. Sellers would list with him at too high a price and then beat him up for not selling the home. This pattern caused George to lose his self-esteem and made it difficult for him to keep himself up. He was struggling at this time to stay in the real estate business. So, for his benefit, I did a class on "Ten Strategies to Get it Priced Right." However, George didn't attend the class. The next day, I told George he'd missed a great session. (I did not ask him where he'd been. I did not tell him he should have been there.) George looked shocked. He said he had intended to come to the class, but, because our secretary didn't remind him personally the day before, he missed the class. It was our secretary's fault! Sure. Our secretary was disturbed about being blamed for something she wasn't responsible for. So, she told George she felt his blame was unfair. He apologized. Later, I spoke with George about the incident. He said that because I put him on the spot, he had to find somebody to blame. This isn't the first time this "pass the blame" has happened with George. My concern, as I expressed to George, was that, even when he's right about someone not carrying out his task, if it gives him a reason to fail, he feels "unempowered." He's unwittingly taking the responsibility for success out of his own hands. I asked him to consider if this was a pattern in his life. He told me it was. Then, I asked him if he could find a way to be "empowered" in situations. That is, even if someone else doesn't carry through, George must believe he's resourceful enough and powerful enough to influence the outcome he wants.

Do you have this pattern? In real estate, it's a dangerous pattern to have. There are so many ways that others can let you down, not cooperate, and seemingly sabotage your success, that you can easily give them the *power* for your success. In doing so, you're letting go of your accountability for your own destiny. That's one example of letting the habits of your attitude manage you. Unless George (and all of us) get control of that attitude, that pesky little attitude will cause us to fail.

Your Attitude Is a Living, Breathing Manager

In real estate, you actually have *two* managers—(1) your broker and (2) the manager in your head. One has much more influence on our success than the other. Now, I suppose you think that real estate managers have a great deal to do with someone's success. Having been a manager for a decade, I wish I could tell you that's true. However, your exterior real estate manager has much less to do with your success than your interior manager—that little manager in your head, the one talking to you all the time, all day! After all, that manager *is* with you all day.

He's commenting on every move you make. (I don't want to be accused of being sexist. Make your voice a "she" if you want. . . .) Are most of his comments positive or negative? For almost all of us, most of the comments are negative. Now, granted, sometimes our interior manager compliments us about an action we just took that worked—once. But mostly, he or she comments on all the things that didn't work out for us. Does he or she give us these comments once? No. Our mind manager sounds like a broken record, telling us over and over the same negative message. Studies show we actually play those same negative messages 20 or 30 times before we get tired of hearing them! Here's one danger. Because our minds automatically and naturally play those negative messages over and over, we actually *start believing them.* Here's another danger. We generalize those messages from those repetitious negative comments to conclusions about our career in real estate. Once we decide that we believe those messages, we've talked ourselves out of real estate.

Let's look at an example of how we transfer a real estate activity into a reason to quit real estate: Susan goes to an open house on Sunday. She's excited to meet the people. She's prepared, having studied the area, talked with the sellers, and created promotional materials for her use. Then, the people start coming in.

The first people say they're just looking. Not knowing what to say to keep the conversation going at that point, Susan says, "Then, just look around. I'll be happy to answer any questions." The next couple tells Susan they're not ready to work with an agent. Throughout the afternoon, as Susan politely tries to open a conversation, people keep throwing barriers at her. Susan gets no appointments. As she picks up her signs, she becomes angry at the people who were just using her time. She plays those negative comments over and over in her mind. She berates herself for not being able to control the conversation. She wonders why the lookers aren't polite enough to engage in a conversation with her. Then, Susan starts getting frustrated about the real estate business. Maybe it's not for her. She's nice; she's prepared. Why won't people work with her? Now, her mind manager is really working on her, telling her all the reasons why real estate is not for her—over and over. By the time Susan gets home, she's convinced herself that real estate is just not for her.

What do you think was going on in the scenario above? As some of you were reading the description, you were saying to yourself, "Susan wasn't really prepared." You're right. Susan had the materials, but she didn't have some critical *skills* to control the conversations to a mutually rewarding end. What skills? The sales communication skills to get past the barriers those people were throwing up. To expect Susan to get appointments at an open house without having practiced and perfected those skills is as futile as a musician trying to play a concerto in front of thousands without practicing. But, then, why did Susan get so frustrated, and draw the conclusion that she wasn't meant for real estate? Because she either

- hadn't had an opportunity to learn the skills, or

- she had discounted the value of becoming skilled at sales communication.

Many times we draw the wrong conclusion from the messages our negative inner manager gives us. We must remember our inner manager may not have all the information necessary to counsel us well.

Inner Managers Try to Protect

If you knew that, to get better at what you were doing, you had to expend great effort and take great risk, would you do it? You might, but your inner manager doesn't want to let you! Tell you what I mean. Your inner manager's most important job is to protect you. Another word, by the way, for your inner manager, is your *subconscious*. Bless his or her heart. He or she is trying to protect you against expending effort and taking risk because those could be, in his or her mind, dangerous to you.

Have you ever known someone whose weight was jeopardizing her health? I had a friend—from grade school years—who became very heavy as a teenager. Her doctor, relatives, and friends all urged her to lose weight because they loved her and cared about her well-being. She tried to go on diets, but she seemed to sabotage herself. She died at twenty, brought on by the strain caused by all that extra weight.

Why doesn't a person do what's good for him? Because his inner manager, his subconscious, is doing the best to protect that person from *change* and *risk*. When the person starts to reject a chocolate sundae, the inner manager says, "Go ahead. It is so comforting. You deserve to be comforted. It's safer to stay the way you are." Because that inner manager has lived with us throughout our life, he or she thinks we are always driven by the same motivators. If we decide we want to be driven by different motivators, our inner managers just don't get the message easily.

Inner managers are well-meaning, ill-informed. When we make a change in our lives, like going into real estate, we must remember to tell our inner manager! If we don't, our inner manager thinks his or her job is to keep protecting us—to keep the status quo. Anything that causes us to change, and to take risk, is going to get many negative comments from our inner manager.

Let's go back to Susan and her open house experience. If Susan is like most agents, she has had some sales training. She probably sat through a class on holding open house, or answering objections. During that class, her inner manager was probably whispering, "You don't need this information or these skills. People will be nice to you without your risking learning new communication skills. If you learn these skills, you may get a customer. You don't really want to risk getting a yes from a potential customer, do you? If you get a yes, you'd have to figure out how to sell that person a home. More risk. Don't start. Just ignore this sales communication information. It would likely make you a manipulative salesperson, and it probably doesn't work anyhow."

Who's really teaching you sales courses?   From teaching sales skill workshops for many years, I know what your inner managers are telling you. In fact, I'm convinced that, in most cases, the inner manager teaches the course! Why? Because, although most sales courses are full of effective, proven skills, few agents actually put these skills to work. Instead of taking risk, risking change, and growing into real estate skills communication, the attendees let their inner manager teach the class. More importantly, they let the inner managers draw the conclusions. These conclusions guarantee that the students won't become good salespeople. The following are comments that I've heard during the class from the attendees. Actually, these aren't really comments from the *consciousness* of the attendees, they're really comments from their inner managers:

- "That won't work in my area."
- "I tried that once."
- "You expect me to ask questions that would get a 'no.' "
- "If you expect me to be a pushy salesperson. . . ."
- "I just give them the address, if that's what they want."
- "I don't want to ask questions. That would be intrusive."

I don't teach manipulative, old-style communication skills. I do teach how to help a *real customer* through the decision-making process. Even with that distinction, most agents' inner managers just won't let them become salespeople! Then, they, like Susan, go to an open house without having developed the sales communication skills necessary to be a professional. They fail because they drew the wrong conclusion about their lack of success in open house. Look into your past experiences in sales. Are there sales skills you rejected that could be helping you with open houses and floor time? Go back to your notes and adopt three new techniques a week for the next four weeks. You'll be amazed at how you'll start ordering your attitude around—and how amazed and pleased you'll be with your new skills—and success.

Developing YOU

Remember when you were a kid. Did you ever want to take part in a sport, or learn a musical instrument? Or did you want to start a venture or an adventure? Why did you want to do it? What did your parents say when you told them what you wanted to do? How strong was your motivation to do it? Did you convince your parents? Did you actually start? Did you keep going? What happened when, to get better, you had to devote more energy, time, and interest to it? Looking back at your life in this area will tell you a lot about your intuitive sense about yourself. It will tell you how much belief you have in yourself, how much tenacity, how much ability to take direction from someone else to get better. It will tell you how willing you are to take risk and to change. Now, fast forward to real estate. Have you taken your intuition, body, and soul into the business like you did in this youthful venture? If not, you need to have a serious talk with your inner manager. He may be stopping you from "acting naturally." That talk might sound like this:

> *Now, Joan (you named your inner manager), I know we've been together a long time. You've done a good job overall giving me advice. However, you're kind of in the dark ages about me now. I want to be successful in this new adventure, real estate. Remember when you supported me as a kid as I [fill in your adventure]. Well, I need your support now. Quit that negative talk about failing, risk, and change. I'm not as scared as you think I am. Give me some pep talks and some laughs and some real positive strokes, as you did before. I need your positive support, Joan.*

Taking ourselves seriously may be detrimental to our success. When I play the piano, people tell me, "You make it look so easy." Sure. Just playing from the time I was four, practicing many years two to four hours a day, experiencing some exhilarating performances, and some poor ones. Being critiqued and evaluated, sometimes positively, sometimes scathingly, and still continuing to perform. Easy. I think the reason I continued to play was that my early experience was so good, so strong. My inner manager was afraid to really mess with me as a kid. However, the older I got, the more scared I got to perform. The joy started leaving. There seemed to be too much pressure on being good. That inner manager, the *mature one,* started working hard, trying to protect me. I finally had to have some talks with that inner manager. It almost became a verbal arm-wrestling contest! I had to convince my inner manager that performances were "play," not "work," and that the goal was the experience of the performance, not the outcome.

In truth, that inner manager's protective comments never leave a performer. So, to continue performing with confidence, verve, and proficiency, we have to learn to put those comments in context. One of my favorite sayings that helps alleviate the performance pressure is one that band directors tell grade schoolers: "Straight ahead and strive for tone." Nike says "Just do it." Quit thinking about all the things that aren't right and all the things that could go wrong. Give yourself low expectations and, like a kid, just have fun in the experience. Learn by doing.

Reduce your inner manager to manageable proportions. Let's say your inner manager is screaming at you to pay attention and quit trying to sell real estate. Listen, then make that voice sound like Donald Duck. Now, make that voice soft and small. Make it sound indecisive. Make it sound questioning and wimpy. Now, tell it "thanks." You don't need it anymore, because, obviously, it doesn't know what it's talking about!

Use a visual one-two punch to control the inner manager. Here's another exercise to get control of that inner manager, especially for you visual people. Each day for a week, write down everything your inner manager tells you. Remember to write down everything—your inner voice is going to tell you the same negative thing at least ten times. Write the message each *time*. Every day, take that piece of paper, crush it into a ball, and throw it away. During that week, tell yourself 20 positive things each day to neutralize those negative messages. Write those down in a notebook. At the end of every day, read all the comments you have written down. By the end of a week, you will have taught your inner manager a thing or two about how you expect him to converse with you in the future!

It's not what happens; it's what you think about it. There are hundreds of self-help books available. They'll help you discover your motivations, your barriers, and your opportunities. One very insightful book rises even above the category of self-help. It's *Emotional Intelligence*, a very well-written and well-researched new book on another kind of intelligence besides IQ, which the author terms *emotional intelligence*. The author, Daniel Goldman, Ph.D., defines emotional intelligence as those attributes of self-awareness, impulse control, persistence, zeal and self-motivation, empathy, and social deftness. Through studies of human behavior, scientists have discovered that emotional intelligence is a predictor of success or failure in life, a greater predictor than IQ.

In *Emotional Intelligence*, Dr. Goldman talks about the power of *hope* in determining success in life. I've observed, time and time again, the strength of this attribute in successful real estate salespeople. Dr.

Goldman shows, through studies, that people who interpret a failure as proof of long-term failure are right. And, people who interpret a failure as temporary are right. What's your life pattern? Has anyone ever called you a "pollyana?" What do you think of when you read that word? What is that word saying about you? Do you like to be around positive or negative people? Would people call you a positive or a negative person? Do you spend your time discounting the actions of others, or praising their actions? Do you spend lots of your energy critiquing others or creating situations for your personal success? How much "hope" do you have?

Retrain your mind. We've already shown you several ways to remind your inner manager to treat you more nicely. One of the keys is for that inner manager to start talking to you again like he did when you were a kid. For some reason, as we get older, those inner managers just get more negative and punitive. Where does that come from? Maybe from our life experiences. As kids, we have natural optimism. If our early experiences beat it out of us, though, it's a real challenge to bring it back. The older we get, the more information we have to critique everything. Generally, we're hardest on ourselves. However, tough-minded, determined people are able to retrain their minds. That's what it takes to succeed in real estate. Are you tough-minded enough, confident enough, and determined enough to teach your inner manager a thing or two at this stage?

Adult conversation frequently helps the negative inner manager retain credibility. Just listen to your conversation during the day. How many of the comments given to you are negative? How many positive? No wonder we learn, unless we're really stupid (well, someone who hated pollyannas would make that comment, wouldn't they. . .) to pay attention to all those negative comments. After all, if the majority of people we're around are saying them, they must be true. Agents frequently tell me that they won't tour properties with certain groups of agents, because the talk is always so negative. By the time the agent gets out of the car, he's convinced himself he should get out of real estate.

What kind of talk? Well, it usually starts with the comments about overpriced homes. Then, it continues to the behaviors of agents—especially those who are successful! Then, the group starts on their own office, the manager, the equipment, the negative feeling in the office (no wonder). Next time you get yourself into one of those cars, do this. Tell the group that you're feeling nauseous for some reason. Would they please stop so you can get a breath of fresh air? Quickly, the group will forget to sing those negative songs and become solicitous (also afraid you'll throw up on them). Then, as you get out, breathe deeply and comment on the beauty of the scenery. You'll have accomplished two things. You'll feel better—and they'll all feel better. Breaking the cycle of negativity is critical to your own well-being and success. If you can help others break their cycles, you're even more powerfully affecting your life—and theirs.

Developing competency cures a negative attitude. Some people think that we must change our attitude before we can change our performance. From studying performance over a lifetime, I believe that we can best cure a negative attitude by jumping right in and learning a new skill. In other words, learn the new skill—even with a bad attitude—and then watch the attitude change. Susan's problem, as we saw, was only that she didn't have, or chose not to put to use, sales communication skills. If she had had the skills to control her destiny at the open house, she would've had a completely different conclusion about the outcome. *Competency* in something cures a bad attitude.

What is competency? The ability to perform at some task at certain predefined levels acceptable for success. To develop competency, we must take a risk to perhaps expose the fact that we're new at something. In our first performance of it, we may embarrass ourselves. We may not do that skill perfectly. For an adult, this risk-taking can be daunting. So, our little inner manager tries to protect us from all these possibilities by giving us those "don't try it" messages.

How to develop competency. Real estate success depends upon performing sales behaviors competently and with confidence. If one can change attitude about something by becoming competent at it, it makes sense that we real estate agents would need to understand exactly how to *become competent.* Competency itself implies *skill.* How do we learn to become skilled? Not by observing only. I can't become a competent pianist by just watching and listening to my teacher play the piano. That's just the first step. After I listen and observe, I must try it myself, with my teacher observing me. Then, we both need to review the performance and do it again.

Today, real estate agents are trying to get good at sales by listening or watching. It's very rare that anyone coaches their practice and gives them feedback. Without coaching and feedback, agents probably do not get the performance right. Then, they try out the skill in real life to little effect. No wonder they say, "That didn't work for me." Don't get me wrong. I'm not suggesting that real estate agents are *asking* that they be taught skills in the wrong way. The industry itself must take the brunt of the responsibility for this poor skill development. Unfortunately, the real estate industry is *teaching* skills incorrectly. They're teaching them not as skills (as my piano teacher taught me), but as ideas (just discussing about how to do something). In classes, the teacher simply talks about the skills. Rarely does the teacher even demonstrate the skill. So the students never get the ability to try out the skill and get coached to even higher performance. To become skilled at anything, we must experience *doing the thing*. Here's the model for skill development:

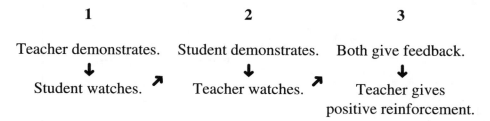

The reason I introduced competency is that I want to give you hope for your career. Now you can review how you've been introduced to sales skills. You can see why you haven't been able to grasp the needed skill to control situations. This lack of control obviously affects your attitude. So, competency is very important to your success. I rate sales skills as second only to prospecting in importance for sales success. If you find you need more competency in sales skills, find a good workshop where you can hear and see demonstrations of sales skills. In this workshop, you should have a chance to try out the skills yourself with a coach, getting feedback until you develop high competency.

Sales skill competency is the first in a positive chain of events. It's thrilling when you learn competency, for it leads you to confidence, better attitude, and success. And, as I've said before, the best motivator to sell is to sell (Figure 3.1)!

Summary

It's not you that's sabotaging your success, it's your out-of-date, misinformed inner manager. Get a grip on that little fellow through acknowledging his messages. Then, ask him to help you change them. Finally, recognize and accept that it's one's competency at something that determines one's attitude about it. Go get sales competency. Take the energy, determination, and talent that's *you* to be as tough-minded about being successful in real estate as you were when you were a kid and wanted something badly. Change your attitude with actions, not words.

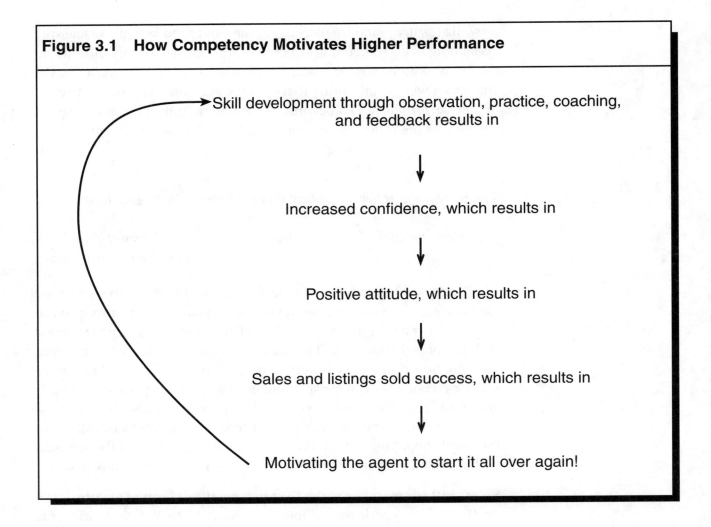

Figure 3.1 How Competency Motivates Higher Performance

Skill development through observation, practice, coaching, and feedback results in

↓

Increased confidence, which results in

↓

Positive attitude, which results in

↓

Sales and listings sold success, which results in

↓

Motivating the agent to start it all over again!

Your Tune-Up for Chapter 3

✓ Read one motivational book per week for the next four weeks. Include the book referred to in this chapter, <u>Emotional Intelligence.</u>

✓ Create a notebook with inspirational articles, sayings, and references. Read it daily for 30 days.

✓ Find the most positive person in your office and get permission to hang around that person for one hour per day for the next week. Ask that person to tell you how he/she maintains his/her positive attitude.

✓ Ask five people in your office how they maintain their positive attitudes. Put to work for yourself one strategy that worked for each of them.

4

Jump Start Your Career to Success

In my survey prior to writing this book, I asked multimillion dollar producers how experienced agents create a low-producing career. Interestingly, most of the respondents cited lack of prospecting as the culprit for low production. Here are a few of these top-producers' observations:

- "They don't prospect daily." Nada Sundermeyer, sales associate
- "They stop prospecting; they spend too much time on follow-up activities once they have a couple of transactions in the pipeline." Anne Bradley, sales associate
- "They get busy with active customers and forget to continue calling and mailing to their prospects and sphere of influence." Karen McKnight, sales associate

The Slump Pattern

In this same survey, I asked what caused agents to fail in their first year. Generally, my respondents named prospecting. Then, I asked what caused agents to go into a slump. The respondents stated that the answer was the same as it was to question one.

What exactly is a "slump"? It's a situation where, because the agents aren't selling homes, they get depressed. Their depression leads to negative feelings about themselves, their associates, their office, the business, and their customers and clients. Then, they usually stay away from the office and find things to do that make them feel good. This, of course, is the beginning of the end of their careers. I think slumps are created as a result of the kind of extension of a sales cycle pattern the agents created for themselves from the beginning.

Let me show you two contrasting "sales patterns." The first, Figure 4.1, shows the success sales pattern. Notice that prospecting activities are continuing even when the agent is also following up on a sale. That assures a constantly replenished supply of prospects, so sales don't dry up. Figure 4.2 shows the sales failure pattern. Notice the differences. In this pattern, there's little prospecting, which results in a sale only after a long period of time. Then, during follow-up, no sales-generating activities are occurring. The result is a low-producing career. You might term this approach "slow and easy." From my observations, it seems that, if the agent didn't prospect as a new agent, he created a low-producing career. During the agent's first year, he may not get too alarmed because he's not making lots of money—after all, some new

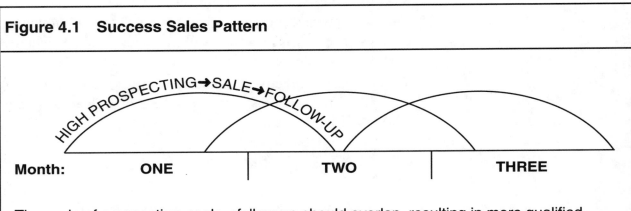

Figure 4.1   Success Sales Pattern

HIGH PROSPECTING→SALE→FOLLOW-UP

Month: ONE   TWO   THREE

The cycle of prospecting→sale→follow-up should overlap, resulting in more qualified listings and buyers, sales, and listings sold. The result is good attitude and motivation.

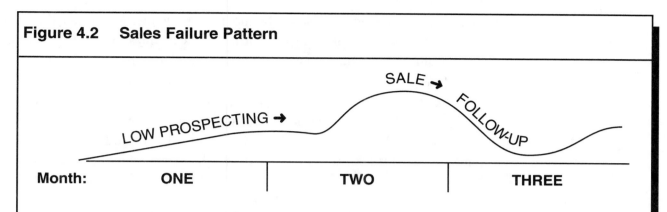

Figure 4.2   Sales Failure Pattern

This pattern of low prospecting, a sale only after a long period of time, and no prospecting activities during follow-up creates a low-producing career. The end result is bad attitude and low motivation.

agents don't expect to make much their first year. And, he may have flashes of production, due to a fast market or just plain dumb luck. However, the agent who doesn't actively and aggressively proactively prospect in the first year creates a certain long-term career activity pattern. I call that the peaks and valleys pattern (Figure 4.3). The agent doesn't see this as a pattern, especially if there are several low producers in his office. He just thinks his lack of production is a matter of really bad luck, bad market, or uncooperative buyers and sellers. It's not just a random event. It's a way of doing business. It's a low-producing *pattern*, and it elicits dangerous mood swings. As top-producer Rick Franz observes:

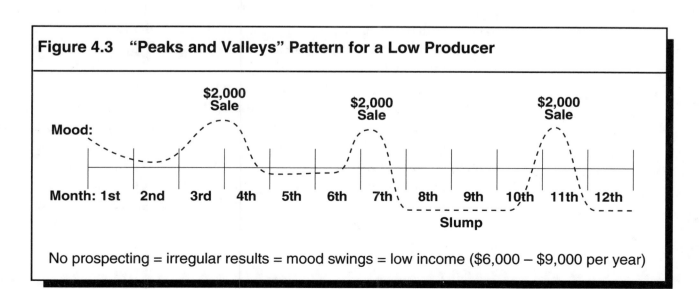

Figure 4.3   "Peaks and Valleys" Pattern for a Low Producer

No prospecting = irregular results = mood swings = low income ($6,000 – $9,000 per year)

- "Experienced agents are bound to experience an up and down business when they're just waiting for the business to come to them rather than going out after it daily."

After all, over time, if the agent only sells a home every three months, the agent has lots of months, weeks, and days when he's depressed! Then, he sits around waiting for something good to happen. The peaks and valleys pattern has been developed. And, like all bad habits, it's a hard pattern to break. But, at least, if that slump pattern is happening to you, you know now that it is a pattern. You can watch for the warning signs of a slumped business:

- Little proactive prospecting
- Waiting for something good to happen
- Putting anyone in your car (any activity is better than none . . .)
- Listing any home, no matter what the price or motivation of the seller (any activity is better than none . .)
- Blaming the market, your office, customers, and clients for your lack of success
- Dropping out, dropping back, and finding other ways besides real estate success to feel good about yourself

The Instant Cure for a Sales Slump

The bottom line: A sales slump is caused when the salesperson stops prospecting. The cure is to start prospecting. Go out and talk to 100 people a week for four weeks. Qualify them. Find the best to work with to help them buy a home. Find the best to help them sell their home. The cure for the slump feeling, depression, is a sale. And, it all starts when you start talking to people. "Wait a minute," you say. You want to pick the best sources of contacts, find the right things to say, know when to call, etc., etc., etc. Well, those considerations are all well and good. And, we'll get to them in this chapter. But, if they stop you from prospecting, they're probably your inner manager trying to protect you from risk and rejection—or even a successful career in real estate. Instead of letting that inner voice slow you down, try acting like you did when you were a child. Get into action before you can talk yourself out of it. Tell that inner manager to be quiet and let you get on with life! Just do it. Then refine it.

The Numbers Game

What are your numbers? Here's a concept I introduced in my book, *How about a Career in Real Estate*. It's the sales cycle (Figure 4. 4). It shows how the progress toward dollars starts when we talk to people (prospect), and it continues only when we continue those sales actions that lead to the dollars. Obviously, the more numbers we complete in each of the sales processes, the better our chances are of getting paid. The *faster* we complete the cycle, the more chance we have of getting

Figure 4.4   The Sales Cycle

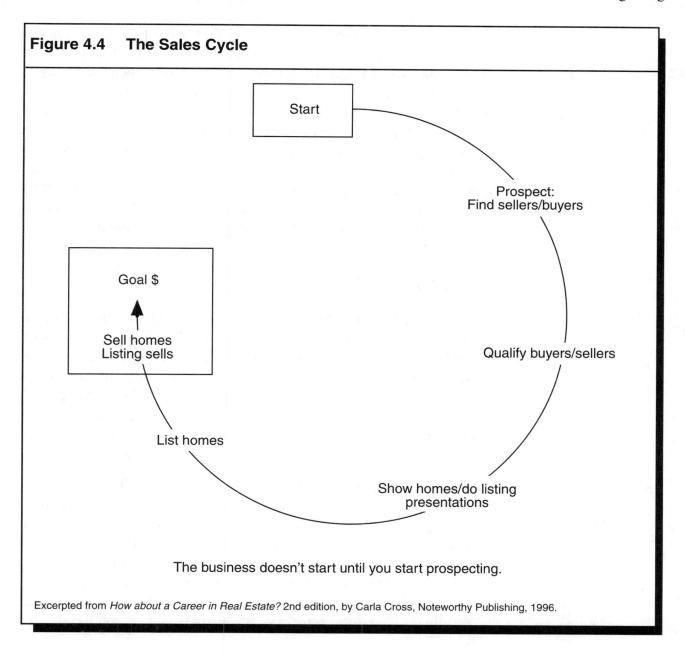

The business doesn't start until you start prospecting.

Excerpted from *How about a Career in Real Estate?* 2nd edition, by Carla Cross, Noteworthy Publishing, 1996.

paid. In order to identify this cycle as a career success pattern, we must first recognize the concept, and then do the activities long enough and fast enough to create a habit of this sales cycle.

Because of its importance to sales success, I think the concept should be introduced to people *before* they become salespeople. Otherwise, when people become agents, they can easily get lost in all the "get ready" activities. The activities they engage in regularly are not sales activities, they're administrative activities. Simply, new agents fail because they don't talk to enough prospects fast enough to get a sale—before they become depressed! They proceed too slowly through the sales cycle, even to identify it as a process.

The important idea here is *time*. To feel like we're on track in any endeavor, we must become successful in a time frame that meets our expectations and keeps us motivated. For the new agent or the agent pulling himself out of a slump, that means that *big numbers prospecting* is key. Let me show you how these numbers add up to sales through time. I've devised a time line that helps agents see, in black and white, how their activities are related to the size of their paychecks every month. It's a prototype plan for an agent who wants to sell one home per month, and is starting with no prior business. Figure 4.5, From Activities to Results, shows how an aggressive prospecting plan will lead to specific results—and when. You can see how the numbers add up through time to sales and listings sold.

Let's Look at Your Numbers

Go back three months in your schedule. Add up all the sales calls you made each week. Put them on the time line in Figure 4.6. Now, working up the time line and working through time, put the numbers you created for listing presentations, sales showings, listings, sales, listings sold, and closings. That's now a snapshot of your business. It shows how you're creating the results you're getting. Now, compare your numbers to those in Figure 4.5. Do you see discrepancies between your time line and that of Figure 4.5? Where are they?

Success ratios.   The time line and success ratios in Figure 4.5 are for a new agent. If you work your best sources of business as an experienced agent, you'll earn better "success ratios" than this agent. What are *success ratios*? The number of sales calls it takes you to get an appointment; the number of appointments it takes you to get a listing or a showing; the number of listings and showings it takes to get a listing sold or a sale. Why will your ratios be better than those of a new agent? You already have some prior clients who think you're wonderful—and

Figure 4.5   From Activities to Results (Prototype Plan)

1. Estimate your activities and when they will create income. *Start with Face-to-Face Contacts.

Activity / Income

Month	1	2	3	4	5	6	7	8	9	10	11	12	Totals
Closings				1	1	1							
Sales		1	1	1	1	1							
Listings Sold				1	1	1							
Listings Secured	1		1		1								
Showings	3	3	8	8	8	8							
Listing Presentations	2	2	2	2	2	2							
Face-to-Face Contacts	400	300	200	100	100	100							

2. Tally your expenses per month. Log in your projected earnings and "paids."

	1	2	3	4	5	6
Business Expenses	1,149	748	818	748	888	818
Earned Income (written)	0	1,500	1,500	0	3,000	3,000
Paid Income (closed)	0	0	0	1,500	1,500	1,500
Profit per Month	($1,149)	($748)	($818)	$752	$612	$682

Figure 4.6 From Activities to Results

1. Estimate your activities and when they will create income. *Start with Face-to-Face Contacts.

Activity / Income

Month	1	2	3	4	5	6	7	8	9	10	11	12	Totals
Closings													
Sales													
Listings Sold													
Listings Secured													
Showings													
Listing Presentations													
Face-to-Face Contacts													

2. Tally your expenses per month. Log in your projected earnings and "paids."

	1	2	3	4	5	6	7	8	9	10	11	12	Totals
Business Expenses													
Earned Income													
Paid Income													

| **Profit per Month** | | | | | | | | | | | | | |

many more real estate business contacts than the new agent. The best sources of business are those people who already trust you and are willing to refer more business to you.

Learning success by the numbers. Generally, the agent's first introduction to sales by the numbers is in his training school. Unwittingly, training schools can mislead agents by the way they teach this sales numbers game. In my opinion, they teach the concept backwards and incompletely. They start with the *end goal* the agent wants, in terms of money, Then, they show the agent how to work from yearly goals back to number of transactions per month. That's it. The agent still doesn't know how to translate those sales results to daily activities. Unfortunately, then, agents jump to the conclusion that those sales will accrue if they show up at the office.

Now that I'm out of training school, what do I *really* do to get started? Somehow, agents don't believe that the business planning ideas they got in training school are relevant to their businesses. I think it's because, as I explained above, the business planning course is frequently taught as long-term and abstract. Also, reality hasn't set in yet, so the students don't accept the fact that, somehow, they must find someone to talk to about real estate if they ever want to sell someone something! Then, agents escape training school and go to their office. They sit around waiting for someone to tell them what to do. (Of course, the manager thinks the new agents know what to do, when to do it, how to do it, and why to do it, because the agents went to training school.)

I conclude that the new agents don't need long-term goal setting nearly as much as they need to know *what to do on Monday—and why.* They need to know how to prioritize the myriad of activities they can do into some orderly fashion. They need to grasp the sales cycle. They need to work out a daily plan that will assure the kind of monthly and yearly goals they want. When we don't introduce sales by the numbers properly in training schools, we mislead agents into the wrong job description. I've included this observation about how new agents get started, because I know thousands of you reading this book started that way. Now, you're searching for a different way to do your business. To help you, I've made the four-week plan for fast sales success (see Chapter 10). Follow it faithfully, and you'll teach yourself the concepts in successful sales by the numbers.

When Expectations Aren't Met

I asked hundreds of agents how much money they expected to make in real estate. They, of course, had already told their managers their expectations during their interviews. Then, I asked these agents how they got the idea that this was the amount they would make. The answers were both amusing and alarming. First, the largest group of agents said they expected to make at least $40,000 to $70,000 their *first* year in real estate. (The average REALTOR® in the United States makes about $24,000—for all years in the business.) I also asked these agents where they got the idea about the income. Here are some of the more frequently given comments:

- "My manager said I could."
- "My friend seems to do real well."
- "I am going into real estate to double my income."
- "I have to make that much to pay my bills."

Out of the hundreds of agents I surveyed, only a few had any idea of the work required to create that kind of income their first year in real estate. In my opinion, by our interview methods and training systems, we're leading new agents to set up a business plan for failure. You know how ludicrous it is for an agent to say they expected to make $50,000 in real estate "because his manager said he could!" You may have experienced the same kind of well-meaning, but misleading conversation as a new agent. I'm convinced that this approach causes some very good people to fail in the business.

Here's that important word again, *time.* By the time agents figure out that attaining their earning goal has little to do with *saying it*, and all to do with *prospecting toward it*, they may be out of time, money, and motivation. The reason that I included the information above is to give you an opportunity to review your thoughts about income prior to entering the business. Who gave you information about income potential? Were expectations set up that, when unrealized, caused you to become demotivated, depressed, and anxious? With the information and four-week program in this book, you can readdress old ideas, get new information, and plan greater success.

The Big Picture

I read over these passages and knew that I'd drive you detail people crazy if I didn't give you a planning grid for projecting out a year in your business. Many of you while in training schools have done part of this. The difference in this grid and many of the grids I've seen from training schools across the nation is that this one does get to the nitty-gritty of daily activities. You can use this plan to actually set up your daily sales activities in your daily planner. In Figure 4.7, Joan's Yearly Goals

Figure 4.7 Joan's Yearly Goals Translated to Monthly Goals and Activities

1. Set your monthly expectations

Your $ expectations this year

$$\boxed{\$ \quad 24,000} \quad \div \quad 12 \quad = \quad \boxed{\$ \quad 2,000}$$

Monthly expectations in $

2. Translate $ to "Units"*

Monthly expectations in $

$$\boxed{\$ \quad 2,000} \quad \div \quad \boxed{\$ \quad 2,000} \quad = \quad \boxed{1/2 \quad | \quad 1/2}$$

Your $ earnings/sale per listing sold

Monthly unit goal

Listings Sold   Sales

* Units are numbers of listings sold/sales.

3. Plan activities to meet

	Month 1	2	3	4	5	6
Listings Sold	0	0	1	0	1	0
Listings Taken	1	0	1	0	0	1
Listing Appointments	4	4	4	4	4	4
Sales	1	1	0	1	0	1
Showing Appointments	8	8	8	8	8	8
Contacts (From 4 week plan)	400	300	200	200	200	200

	Month 7	8	9	10	11	12
Listings Sold						
Listings Taken						
Listing Appointments						
Sales						
Showing Appointments						
Contacts						

Figure 4.8 Your Plan: Monthly Goals and Activities

1. Set your monthly expectations

Your $ expectations this year

$ [   ] ÷ 12 =

Monthly expectations in $

$ [   ]

2. Translate $ to "Units"*

Monthly expectations in $

$ [   ] ÷

Your $ earnings/sale per listing sold

$ [   ] =

Monthly unit goal

Listings Sold	Sales

* Units are numbers of listings sold/sales.

3. Plan activities to meet

	Month 1	2	3	4	5	6
Listings Sold						
Listings Taken						
Listing Appointments						
Sales						
Showing Appointments						
Contacts (From 4 week plan)						

	Month 7	8	9	10	11	12
Listings Sold						
Listings Taken						
Listing Appointments						
Sales						
Showing Appointments						
Contacts						

Translated to Monthly Goals and Activities, I've used that same prototype plan that you saw in the timeline earlier in this chapter (Figure 4.5). This time, it starts with the end goal in mind and works backward. Figure 4.8 is a blank grid for you to use to translate your end goals into daily activities. Warning. Warning. Don't use this grid unless you're willing to compute the activities and put them into your daily plan. I don't want you deceiving yourself into believing that writing your goals and figuring out how many sales and listings sold it takes will assure you get there. No. It just assures you know how to figure this out!

Now is not the time to worry about the big picture. You want to jump-start your career, right? Okay. Let's get out the jumper cables. Let's not read the instruction book on the 12,000 mile checkup. You haven't driven 12,000 miles. You can't get that baby started! That's your problem. So, let's just start at the beginning, and do it. Almost all agents who want to dramatically increase their business have a prospecting problem. The other problems are much smaller. Don't worry, though. We'll handle those too.

How your weekly plan will assure you change your career for the better. So that you can easily put your career on track, I've created a four-week plan in Chapter 10 in this book. It incorporates the ideas in this book into a realistic, success-proven plan. To start the plan, I've recommended the number of sales calls in specific areas you want to accomplish, using the activity grids and timelines provided. Then, you'll keep track of your successes with these timelines. After doing this for a month, you'll have a clear picture of how you are achieving success. You'll have an accurate picture of your success ratios, so you know, in the future, how much prospecting it will take you to create the results you want from this business. In other words, you'll have learned the self-management tools critical to success in the real estate business. The result is a new job description.

Playing the Numbers by Prospecting and Following Up

Prospects are everywhere. Which ones are best for me? Are you convinced that jump-starting your career depends on prospecting? I hope so, because the whole matter of your success depends on that belief. But, who to prospect and how? Well, I'm only going to tell you if you promise me that this information won't slow you down. I know some agents who spend six months researching a particular market to find out whether that market would be a good one for prospects. In the meantime, someone has just listed four homes in that market! So, don't spend too much time researching the possibilities.

Who were your best prospects this past year?   In some ways, it's easier to help an experienced agent create a much stronger business than to help a new agent get started. Why? Because the experienced agent has seen the results of a bad business plan. Intellectually, the principles I've explained here are so logical and commonsensical that the new agent says, "Well, okay. That's easy to understand. Get to the hard part." But, experienced agents realize these principles aren't hard to understand. They're hard to put into action. Prospecting is easily explained. As a skill, though, it's challenging to do. Unfortunately, though, by the time agents get six months in the business, their inner manager has convinced them that the reasons they haven't done as well as they expected had nothing to do with prospecting, and everything to do with *everything else.* That inner manager again—protecting us from a career in sales.

How to use your track record to steer you.   The good news is that the experienced agent has a track record, a benchmark, to analyze. In this book, I'm showing you how to compare your prior record to benchmarks for success—and to make the changes in your program to match a "success career." The first principle in sales is to prospect. Now, you have a track record, so you can refine your prospecting program for the *best sources of leads.* First, let's look at your track record. Complete Figure 4.9, A Review of Your Business. It will assist you in getting a clear picture of where your business came from in the past year. It's very important to complete this analysis, for we'll build on your successes for better career results.

The results of reactive versus proactive sources of business.   Do you take floor time? Do you hold open houses? These are forms of "reactive" prospecting. That means that agents receive prospects by sitting in one place and waiting for them. Proactive means agents go out and find leads by phone calling and personal visits. In truth, all of us in sales would rather wait for someone to come to us than to have to go out and find business. And, there's nothing wrong with these prospecting methods. Nothing wrong, that is, unless you got more than 30 percent of your business from them last year. Why? Because, the more you wait for business, the more precarious your opportunities to earn money in this business become. I did a study with experienced agents and found that the lower their production, the more they depended on leads coming to, or finding, them (Figure 4.10). In other words, low producers wait for business to come to them. High producers go out and find business. Look at your analysis from Figure 4.9. Which kind of business did you create? Knowing that low-producing agents receive

Figure 4.9   A Review of Your Business

Sales _____   Listings taken (LT) _____

Listings sold (LS) _____   % of LT to LS _____

Average time on market for your listings: _____ (Breakdown by price range if desired)

% of sales price to list price for your listings _____   Number of new listings sold _____

Number of resales sold _____   Number of resale listings sold _____

Number of new homes sold _____

Origination of Buyers/Sellers		
	Buyers	Sellers
Reactive prospecting		
Floor time		
Open houses		
Proactive Prospecting (Segmented by Target Market)		
Old Customers/Clients		
First-Time buyers		
Move-up buyers		
Transferees		
Empty-Nesters		
Geographical farm		
Prior business contacts		
Builders		
Other:_____		

Of these sellers, which market gave you the most sold listings?

☞ **Keep exploiting these markets. They're your most effective.**

Figure 4.10 Results of a Reactive versus Proactive Career

Which career do you want? The following are descriptions of the kind and number of activities agents do to create certain "levels" of business. These observations are taken from analyses of particular agents' daily schedules and their results. For contrast, I've given labels to each of three types: Licensee (low producer), Agent (mid-producer), Professional (good producer).

"Licensee": 1/2 Transaction per Month

To generate business:	Reactive Activities only: Floor time & Open house 20 leads = 1/2 transaction monthly

"Agent": 1 to 1 1/2 Transactions per Month

To generate business:	1/2 Reactive and 1/2 Proactive activities
Reactive:	Floor time and open house = 1/2 transaction
Proactive:	100 contacts a month = 1 transaction

"Professional": 2+ Transactions per Month

To generate business:	1/4 Reactive and 3/4 Proactive
Reactive:	Floor time and open house = 1/2 transaction
Proactive:	200 contacts a month = 2 transactions

The more proactive prospecting done, the higher the income.

---

most of their business from waiting for and high-producing agents receive most of their business by going to get it can help you understand how you've created your results.

If the business came to the agent, it was probably "loved and left."   Another principle I found in studying high and low producers was that low producers failed to maintain a business relationship with their buyers and sellers *after* the closing. The result was that they garnered few referrals. We agents know, though, that working with someone referred to us is much more pleasant than working with strangers. Why, then, wouldn't the experienced agents want to gain referrals? It all comes from their misconceptions about how business is created. Agents who depend on reactive prospecting methods look at their role in real estate as a passive one. For example, because they did nothing to find the buyer, they don't bother or have time to establish rapport. (These reactive agents think that the only good buyer is the one with cash in hand, who points out the home he wants to buy. By the way, this "qualified" homebuyer never has a home to sell. This situation would be too complicated to reactive agents.) The sale happens. The buyer leaves. The agents wait for the next one.

What's the service worth?   How much is a movie ticket today? Seven dollars? It's surely not as much as a real estate commission check! Yet, too many agents treat their customers like we're treated at the motion picture ticket window. You can almost hear the agents yell, "Next in line." This attitude toward the customer is created from the misperception by agents that this is an easy business, based on people coming to us, ready, willing, and able to purchase, that our job is to wait for an easy buyer and do the barest necessities to get a commission check. The sad result about this reactive attitude is the perception created about real estate agents in the mind of the buyer. Because of the approach of the agents, the buyer concludes that the agents don't care enough about buyers to really find out their needs, tackle any difficulties, or keep in touch with them after closing. These same agents are the agents who don't understand why these buyers, when they're ready to sell, don't pick up the phone and call them!

Your best source of business.   So, you're ready to proactively prospect. Which source of business will have the highest payoff for you? The ones who already think you're wonderful! Who are these people? The people you've sold homes to, or sellers whose home you listed and it sold. (Forget it if you think you're getting referrals from people whose homes you listed, but didn't sell.) But, you know people only move about once in seven years (and they're moving less and less frequently). Let's say you've been in the business only three years. If business depends on your "sold" customers and clients, how are you going to force these people to move more often so you can get commissions from them?

You're not. You're looking for *referrals* from these people. After all, if you did a great job for them, who better than you to help their friends? Staying in touch with people who bought and sold with you is good business sense. That's the only way you'll ensure that you will ever work with them again. That's the only way that you'll ensure that you get your best source of business—referrals.

Show first that you care. Studies show that buyers and sellers don't think most agents care much about them. Why? Because, most agents don't even pick up the phone after closing and find out how things are going! If you're in this career to create long-term, ever-increasing business, your objective will be completely different from that reactive agent we discussed earlier—the one who "loved 'em and left 'em." Here's how to start that long-term relationship and to show you care more about that person than just that commission check:

- Say thanks and buy a housewarming gift within three days of closing.
- Call every three days after closing for the first week, to be sure everything's okay.
- Call once a month for the first six months after closing.
- Call, drop buy, and send something to your valued clients at least four times a year.

When has an agent earned a commission? According to a consumer survey, real estate clients said they thought agents were worth the commission they charged *only* when they had followed up consistently over a period of time *after closing*. Love 'em, don't leave 'em. Spending your time and money on people who've paid you for your services is a mark of a professional. After all, what would you think of someone who sold you something (and received thousands in commissions)—and never thought enough of your well-being to call you and find out how you were doing with that product or service? Not very committed. Not very professional. Would you go back to that salesperson or refer someone to him or her?

If it's important to their survival and success, why don't agents stay in touch? I think there are several reasons. There are so many part-time real estate agents who have other things on their mind. There are many noncommitted, reactive agents looking for easy money. Many agents are in and out of the business so fast that their buyers and sellers are "orphaned." As a manager, I've found I've had to try to save our company reputation by assigning orphaned buyers and sellers to an agent in our office. Otherwise, the consumers just think that all that mattered to the agent is that check. They don't know the agents went out of the business—nor do they care.

What we've found, by the way, in calling these orphaned buyers and sellers, is that they are disappointed that *someone* has not cared enough about their interests to keep in touch. I think it's a company's obligation to provide ongoing real estate services to those people who were nice enough to buy and sell with that company. This is a way, too, you can increase your business. When agents leave your office, go to your manager and get a list of their orphaned buyers and sellers. Call those people, and explain that the manager has asked you to keep in touch. They will be thankful and appreciative. You'll gain another source of business, and the industry's image will be maintained—or raised.

Working with referrals is more pleasant.   Much of our meetings with potential buyers and sellers who don't know us is spent in establishing credibility with them. If we can't help them learn to trust us, they won't take our recommendations on pricing the home, creating the offer, etc. Without this credibility, we always feel out of control. Now, contrast that with the experience you've had meeting and working with someone who's been referred to you by a loyal customer. That customer has already given you a real buildup. You're not a stranger to that new client. You're already a credible, believable professional. The new client already feels fortunate to get to work with you! The hard part of your job is over. Because the client already trusts you, you have a much easier time explaining the selling and buying process. The client takes your advice well, and makes a good decision, because you are working in real partnership, not as adversaries. Which relationship do you like?

The opportunity for the best business.   All you have to do to get a client who's easy to work with is to ask your old customers and clients for referrals. Here's the process for asking for referrals:

1. *Tell* your customer you've been thinking about them.
2. *Give* them a real estate update in your area.
3. *Ask* them if they know of anyone interested in that real estate, or of anyone else they know of interested in buying or selling?

To help you further, I've recorded some tips and role-plays on the audiotape. A caveat: Remember to call your old customers and clients because you care about them, not just because you want referrals. When you call, don't always ask for referrals!

Business from old customers is much less expensive than generating new business from strangers.   One of the biggest mistakes experienced agents make is to spend too much money on strangers. They don't know a proven marketing principle: *It costs six to nine times more to get a new customer than to keep an old one.*

In other words, when real estate agents fail to keep in contact with their old customers regularly and ask them for referrals, they cost themselves much more money in personal marketing than they need to spend. I teach business planning to thousands of real estate agents and managers. I ask them how much money they spent on their best source of business last year. They tell me that they've spent $50 to $200—total! Generally, agents need to increase their budgets for this best source. However, I've found that it's difficult to spend thousands of dollars getting lots of business from your best target market, old customers, and clients. In reverse, though, it's easy to spend many thousands of dollars trying to find strangers to work with (in newspaper ads, radio, television, brochures, etc.). The biggest payoff for your marketing dollars is in spending them to re-relate to your old customers and clients—with the objective of referral business. Look at your business plan. Where did you spend the most dollars? What was your payoff?

Recommunicate YOU in print to your most valuable market.   Here are some ideas that successful agents use all over the nation to remind their customers and clients that they are still successful, trustworthy, and that they love referrals:

- Letter at the end of the year thanking them for their support and telling them your accomplishments, and that you couldn't have done it without them
- Regular newsletter article thanking them for their referrals
- Regular newsletter article featuring the new buyers/new sellers that have been referred to you and what they bought (remember to get permission from clients before printing their names and testimonials)
- Letter with thanks and testimonials from those you sold that were referred to you; and who the referring source was

How did you communicate with your best source of business last year?   Businesses internationally, and not just real estate, are discovering that, to avoid great expense and make a profit, they need to get more business from their old customers and clients. In fact, the extension of this principle, *networking,* is the most popular, successful, and profitable form of marketing products and services in the late twentieth century. It's so old it's new again, fortified with the instant communications systems we now have available. To find out how you communicated last year to your best source of business, answer the questions in Figure 4.11.

Figure 4.11   Communicating with Your Old Customers and Clients

How many listings sold and sales came directly from your old customers and clients? How many referrals from them did you get?

How many times, on average, did you call them?

How many mail pieces did you send? How many times did you visit them personally?

Did you ask for the order, a referral, or hope that they would give you one without your asking?

How much money did you spend on them?

Overall, from your actions, how much of your professionalism did you share with them?

What do you think, from your behaviors toward them, they think of you?

Does that perception need to be changed?

List your plans, right now, for contacting your old customers and clients for referrals:

Other target markets and potential. In the four-week plan (Chapter 10), we'll be introducing more sources of business. Some of the sales skills required to make these sales calls will be role-played on the audiotapes. We'll also expand our *networking* idea for additional referrals from people you know. Right now, though, go back to Figure 4.9 and prioritize your other best sources of business besides old customers and clients. As you launch your four-week plan, keep contacting your best markets for more business.

Summary

First, it's a simple business—a sales business. It all starts when we start talking to people. Talking to lots of people is more important to launching or relaunching your career than trying to pick the best markets, the best script, the best flyers, the best *anything*. Letting your inner manager stop you from starting prospecting has to be *not okay with you now.*

As an experienced agent, you have the luxury of already having benchmarks with which to compare success behaviors. Understanding how the numbers work toward creating your success is the first step in effective self-management. With that concept, you're ready to generate more business. Your best source of business is the customers you just sold. Care enough to follow up with them impeccably. It will bring you business, but, most of all, it will bring you joy. You'll develop the confidence of hearing again that you've helped someone make the best decision of their lives. Through talking with these old customers, you'll feel great!

Your Tune-Up for Chapter 4

✓ Complete Figure 4.6, From Activities to Results. Compare it to 4.5. What changes do you want to make in your business plan to achieve the results you want? Create a new plan for yourself, using Figure 4.6 Transfer your business plan to Figure 4.8, Your Plan: Monthly Goals and Activities. You'll get the "big picture" of how your daily activities guarantee your bottom-line results at the end of the year.

✓ Complete Figure 4.11, Communicating With Your Old Customers and Clients. Evaluate your sales effectiveness. Create a new communication plan, with dates, activities, and budget. Put the activities into your daily planner so they're scheduled.

5

Getting Your Career Rolling Without a Major Tune-Up

> *My best promotional dollars spent are keeping in touch with and rewarding past clients, friends, and agents who refer business to me.*
>
> **—Rick Franz, sales associate**

As an experienced agent, you really do have lots of advantages over people new to the business. You have already tackled and conquered the strange language of real estate. You know the areas, the agents, the business systems in your office and the multiple listing service. In addition, you have some "people" advantages—other sources of business. However, they're usually not a part of an experienced agent's business plan. Why? Because those giving advice, managers and trainers in particular, tend to lump all agents together. They give the same advice to experienced agents that they give to new people. But, you're in a different situation. Because you've been in the business, you've made a positive impact on some particular people who can really jump-start your career. So, here are four very effective methods of generating business for you that new agents don't have available:

1. Sellers who didn't list with you

2. Buyers who didn't buy from you

3. Your former business associates

4. Other agents

Pursuing Sellers Who Didn't List with You

You can get business from those who *didn't* "buy" your services from you. In the previous chapter, we explored methods for you to get more business from people who bought from you. In addition, though, there's another great market for you—the people who you've worked with who, for whatever reason, didn't list or buy from you. Let's first look at the seller who didn't list with you. Before we investigate this source, let me remind you of my premise that to build your business in the future you'll list only marketable properties—those properties that will sell in normal market time—so you'll create delighted clients. If you're serious about your career image, you don't want to ruin it with listings that don't sell.

So, with that business principle in mind, I'll assume that you walk away from about half the listing appointments you keep *without a listing*. If you don't list the property, what will happen to it? Some other agent will list the property overpriced. Then, the property will sit on the market for a long time. Finally, the agent either loses the listing or wrestles the seller down in price. No matter what, the agent has lost the goodwill of the seller and can't get referrals. The reason you're willing to walk away, of course, is that your job is to get homes *sold,* not get them *listed.* (In the chapter on the listing process, we'll look at your listing practices and refine them for more powerful listing success.) Before you walk away from that seller, care enough about him to set up a communication system for the future. Okay, I just heard you mutter that, if you kept in contact with the seller, you would be soliciting the listing. Did I say that? No way. I said, "Care enough about the seller to set up. . . ." Did you ever wonder what sellers think of agents who spend hours consulting with them prior to listing, calling them constantly, sending them market information, and then abruptly quit communicating with them when the seller lists with someone else? They may think that all you cared about is getting the listing. Well, is that all you cared about, or do you care enough about the seller to keep him informed on market conditions? Is there a rule that you can't talk to or send a seller market information when the home is listed with another agency? Of course not. What you can't do is try to take that listing away from the other agency. You can't send soliciting information or have soliciting conversations.

When in doubt about what is a "soliciting conversation," or "soliciting material," check with your broker. In my estimation, if you've established a professional relationship with a seller, you have a duty to continue that relationship as a customer service. If you quit all communication, how can the seller remember who you are and send you referrals? So, your objective in continuing that communication with the seller is to obtain referrals from that seller.

Find Out How You Did

And finding out how you did includes learning how you can improve. Many times, when agents don't get the listing, they assume it was because of the price. Instead of assuming, take the opportunity to call the seller. But, don't just call and ask why you didn't get the listing. Demonstrate your caring about your profession—and your interest in the seller—by using a marketing survey. I've provided one for you in Figure 5.1. Be sure to do this survey verbally, so you have another opportunity to demonstrate to the seller your unique marketing approach. Your objective is to show the sellers that you're keeping *their best interests* in mind—not just yours.

Delighted with the service?   Why do people give us referrals? Because they were delighted with the way we treated them. From a seller's view, what is "delightful service?" According to a survey done by *Consumer Reports* a few years ago, sellers rated the service as "high" from their agency and agent only if it accomplished three things:

1. The home *sold.*
2. The home sold *quickly.*
3. The home sold for *close to full price.*

Those were the three main components for high customer satisfaction. Listing agents, though, think that sellers are highly satisfied with the service if they keep in touch during the listing period. Sellers are telling us that, although keeping in touch is an expected service, it's not enough to create high customer satisfaction. To get referrals, the home must have sold quickly at close to full price.

Doing it the old way makes money—but doesn't build a strong business.   Some agents overprice properties, arm-wrestle sellers to get price reductions, and hold listings for a long market time. And these agents make money. So, you argue, those kinds of business methods

---

Figure 5.1 Survey to Sellers You Didn't List

Always use this as a phone or in-person survey.

Concept: You're getting seller feedback on your *marketing plan* (of which pricing is only a part). Your questions reflect your approach to the listing process.

Survey technique: Ask the questions. Listen. Probe for more information. Do not argue. If the seller gives you information you know to be incorrect, or if you want to give the seller more information, make a note and send the seller that information in writing. Seeing is believing. For the next presentation, you'll know you need to put that information in your visual marketing plan when you're competing with certain companies and/or agents.

Introduction: "Mr. and Mrs. Smith, thank you for giving me the opportunity to present my marketing plan to you. I understand you've decided to list with ABC Realty. As part of my business plan, I'm always striving to refine my marketing methods. Would you please give me some feedback, so that I can better serve sellers' needs?"

1. What about my marketing plan appealed to you the most?

2. What about ABC's plan appealed to you?

3. I know sellers expect a sale—in a reasonable period of time. How could I improve my marketing plan to assure sellers I can help them reach their goals?

4. What about my presentation methods seemed effective to you?

5. How could I improve my presentation methods? (visuals, statistics?)

6. How could I have given you more information to make your decision?

7. What are your plans if your listing doesn't sell within your listing time period?

"Thanks so much. I enjoyed working with you. Let's keep in touch. May I put you on my mailing list for my real estate newsletter? It provides lots of information about the area. . . .If you have questions I can answer, please call me. Also, I would appreciate knowing about any people I can help buy or sell in our area. Who do you know that may need my service?"

must be okay, right? Not if you want to build a strong business *for the future*. Those agents are working with old-style, manipulative sales methods. They've been in the business many years and are working with referrals. They've gotten the "line of patter" in their businesses to be able to "explain" why no one previews or shows the listings. Because they do business with people who already know them, they get the benefit of the doubt. But, they don't get that most important marketing component for the twenty-first century: word of mouth networking.

So, if you want to build your business for the future, you must resist the impulse to use the sign on the property for your own good—not the seller's. In every business book written today, the first principle of selling is creating "delighted customers." Think of your own experience as a consumer. Are you more savvy today as a consumer than ten years ago? Is there more information available to you? The old-style manipulative method requires a naive, trusting consumer. It creates some sales from signs and ads, but it's becoming increasingly difficult to sustain over a period of time. Why? Because the consumer has caught on. And, in the future, this kind of manipulative technique will work less and less well. Consumers have learned to ask the right questions. They're going to increasingly choose professionals in every field *through personal and professional references.*

When sellers are not "delighted." How long does it take before sellers become dissatisfied with the service they're receiving from their listing agent? I ask that question to agents across the country. From their experience, they respond, "About a month." So, in a month, if an agent overprices a property, no matter how many ads the agent has run, how many open houses, how many other promotional strategies were completed—the customer's now dissatisfied. Manipulative agents then go into high gear with their "sales spiels," blaming everyone and everything on lack of showings and offers. Still, the customer's dissatisfied. Will that seller give referrals at that point to the listing agent? You can bet not. But, agents who overprice homes are not interested in referrals. Their objective is to keep the seller from cancelling the listing so that they can get the price down, or get buyers from ads and signs, or weaken the seller and get a low offer.

In contrast, *your* objective in a listing presentation is not to get a listing—unless you can get it priced to sell. Your overall objective is to make such a favorable impression that, over time, by keeping in contact with the seller, you'll *receive referrals.* Sometimes you'll even list that property *at the right price* after the sellers become so dissatisfied with the manipulative strategies of the first agent that they refuse to be used and abused any longer. There's a truism in marketing that describes what's going on in the "overpricing scenario": Customers don't know what they're getting—until they don't.

Two approaches to sellers. We've been exploring these two strategies. These are:

1. Old marketing strategy: Get a listing at any price and use the listing sign to get calls ("bait and switch").
2. New marketing strategy: List only well-priced properties to build trust and the reputation as agent who *sells properties.*

Which strategy is easier in the short run? The old marketing strategy. Which strategy guarantees a long-term successful career? Of course, the second. It's not only our individual careers that are at stake. I'm convinced that the whole future of our industry depends on how we treat the customer. I know we must treat the customer with more respect and care than we have in the past. After all, if we agents don't keep the sellers' (and buyers') best interests in mind, we'll be out of business. Now, sellers and buyers can use the Internet to communicate. In the future, when agents don't *help* sellers, but *hinder* them, the sellers will bypass the agent!

A success story. Nada Sundermeyer, one of the top agents in the United States, provides this advice about listing practices. I asked her, "What specific recommendations do you have for the best use of an agent's promotional budget?" Nada's answer: "Get a sold sign on their listings."

Having worked with Nada for several years, I can tell you that's how she built her business. As a new agent, she decided to build on success. She listed only properties that would sell in a short period of time, for close to full price. She created a whole cheerleading section of satisfied, delighted sellers. She used this success to promote herself to other sellers. She encouraged satisfied sellers to promote her services to many other people.

Nada has masterfully combined the concepts of

- telling the truth to the seller,
- having the objective of referrals, not a listing,
- promoting her successes, and
- creating a network of cheerleaders.

Just by deciding to list only marketable properties, you can do the same thing. I'm explaining the concepts throughout this book. All you need do is to adopt this business philosophy and put it to work in the field for great success.

Pursuing Buyers Who Didn't Buy with You

Another great source of business is the buyers you didn't sell. I'll never forget one time when I lost some buyers to another agent who used the old "it will be gone if you don't buy it now" and "I'll take care of your agent." I was furious at having buyers taken from me! Then, when I calmed down, I thought over the information I had given the buyers. I decided I could've done a better job at the beginning of the relationship by explaining how I work and how other agents work. In fact, it's because of these situations that I developed the systems that I use today. (If you need a presentation on controlling buyers, see my *List the Buyer* package, in the Reference section of this book.) In a later chapter, we'll investigate strategies for creating long-term customer loyalty. At any rate, these buyers blithely bought the home from the other agent. Still, I kept in touch with them, because I liked and cared about them. Well, as you could guess, the other agent didn't provide good service. After all, agents who want to snag buyers with these old-style manipulative sales methods aren't the kind of agents who care about long-term business relationships. After just a few days, the buyer told me, "I'm so sorry I bought from the other agent. He's a part-timer, doesn't return my calls, and doesn't know what he's doing." I kept in touch with the buyer. Over time, we established a mutually beneficial long-term business relationship. I got four referrals from this buyer because I proved I cared about him. The other agent got only one commission check.

Keep Your Cool to Get Referrals

Here's the situation. The buyers were delighted with your service, even though they didn't buy from you. You can get referrals from them, if you *keep your cool* when you find out the bad news. Helen and Bob— I'll never forget the day I called them to make an appointment and they told me they had bought a home. Now, this is after I had showed them homes for a year and bought them lunch at least once a week. Not only did Helen tell me, during that phone conversation, that she'd bought a home from someone else, she attempted to make me feel better by saying, "Your commission, Carla, would have been only $1,500." Oh, that was comforting, Helen! Well, I had trouble keeping my cool because I thought I had really been taken advantage of. And, deep down, like all of us, I was really mad at *me* (for all the reasons you just thought of).

But, I knew the agent Helen and Bob had bought from, so I guessed they wouldn't like the way they were going to be treated. I also knew they had a home to sell. So, I calmed myself, smiled into the phone, and said, "Good for you. I'm so happy you found the home you wanted. When shall we list your home?" I got an appointment for the listing. Then, I hung up and screamed for a couple of minutes. The end of the story is that the listing sold quickly. The agent who sold them their home never called them after he negotiated the offer. He never called or dropped by after closing. He really loved 'em and left 'em. Not me. Because I'd worked with Helen and Bob for that year, I had a good relationship with them and their son. I really cared about their well-being. I kept in touch. Bob and Helen really saw the difference in our approaches. They sent me five referrals in three years, and they even bought *me* lunch!

Dialogue for Referrals

Okay, you're keeping your cool. You've just found out that the buyers you've been working with just bought from someone else. Now's your chance to prove what you're all about. Here's your dialogue: "I'm happy that you found your dream home. Of course, I'm sorry that it wasn't with me, but, as I told you from the beginning, my job is to make sure you get what you want. I hope my service was helpful to you in choosing the right home for you. Whether I had sold you a home or not, my real objective in working with you is to establish long-term business relationships so that, when someone you know needs to sell or purchase a home, you'll think of me. Let's keep in touch. I provide a newsletter to my clients that gives the latest real estate trends, and I'll be happy to include you on my mailing list. I'll give you a call to touch base every so often, too. If there's any question I can answer, please let me be of help. By the way, who do you know now that needs my help selling or purchasing?"

Pursuing Former Business Associates

Here is the best-kept secret source of prospects—with little competition. How did you make a living before you went into real estate? The people who you got to know in your previous jobs are some of your best sources of business. And, there's little competition from other agents for them. Why are you the best agent for your former colleagues? Because you know the types of personalities in that field. You speak the "lingo." You know the values, the challenges, the trends in that business. And, your former colleagues know you. They know the talents you brought to that business. They have a higher level of trust in you than in someone who doesn't understand their field. My surveys have shown that agents generate more business from their former business colleagues than from their friends. I think it's because your business colleagues already respect you as a business person. So, put these people on your prospecting list. In the four-week plan, you'll have assignments to contact a number of these people weekly.

Pursuing Other Agents—An Untapped Prospect Source

Here's another fabulous source of business: other agents. Smart agents today take full advantage of their opportunities to network with agents in other areas. It pays off. I just got a promotional letter from Nada Sundermeyer, a master agent networker. She received over $200,000 in commission dollars from agents' referrals last year! If you've ever attempted to refer a customer or client, you know it's difficult to find an agent who works like you do. Have you ever referred a buyer or seller to an agent and had a bad experience? Almost all agents have. That either teaches us to never refer to someone or to be careful who we refer to. So, the key in establishing an agent referral network is to inspire agents' confidence in us.

Finding Agents Who Will Refer to Us

There are various ways to find agents who will refer to us. We meet other agents in our

- real estate courses.
- REALTOR® Association meetings and committees, and
- visits to other real estate offices.

Here's how we might open a conversation to ask for referrals: "George, it's been delightful meeting you. Do you have anyone to refer to in my market area? I'd love to be the person you trust your referrals to. And, in return, I will send my referrals to you. What are you looking for in an agent? (Listen and take notes.) Why don't I send you my brochure. It tells you about my specialties and has some comments from clients who've been pleased with my service. I'll also send you comments from agents whom I refer to, and they refer to me."

Notice, I didn't just ask for referrals. I want to find out what's important to that agent, so I can provide the kind of service George wants. I want to know how he wants me to contact the referral, how he wants me to keep in touch with him, etc. In addition, I must give the other agent a reason to be comfortable referring to me.

In contrast, here's the system most agents use. I get a letter once in awhile from an agent who asks me for referrals. "Once" is the operative word here. The agent very rarely sends me a letter more than once. (They don't know the marketing principles of consistency and frequency.) What do I do with all those "one time" letters? The round file. (It takes 9 to 27 times of mailing to get a customer. The agents give up on me before they make an impact!) Do they think I'd just refer my treasured customer to them just because they wrote me a letter—once? From my experiences in referring, I'm too cautious to entrust my customer to someone who sends me a letter—once.

Tell them why you deserve the referrals. The other disturbing part of these letters is that the agent never tells me why I should feel comfortable referring to that agent. Knowing that we have all had bad experiences referring our business, I wonder why agents don't take the time to give me some credibility statements. Notice in the suggested dialogue that I refer to a brochure. It doesn't matter if you have a one-page typed resume or a four-color brochure. What matters is that you've thought ahead and taken the time to create some credibility statements. I'm also impressed by those statements, because I know the agent is serious about his career long-term and is thinking about networking toward long-term business relationships.

The other type of credibility statement should be testimonials from agents who have referred to you. Nothing says "trustworthy" better than those who have had the experience of actually working with you. So, whenever possible, don't say it yourself. Have others say it. Figure 5.2 is a letter that Mallory Shibuya, a very professional agent in my office, created to establish credibility for referrals. It's worked very well for her. Make changes to fit your style. Your manager can also support you by giving you a testimonial letter directed to other agents, relocation directors, etc. Use these letters to establish long-term, networking referral relationships.

Have a system for follow-up communication. I can't tell you the number of times I've referred a customer or client, and never heard back from the agent! That sure makes me confident. And, by the way, it's not my job to call that agent and ask how things are going. The agent is making most of the money. He or she should get in touch with me. If you

Figure 5.2   Sample Letter

Ms. Susan Jones
ABC Realty
1000 First Avenue
Omaha, Nebraska

Dear Susan:

As a fellow CRS, why don't we partner in profits for 1996? In developing my
1996 business plan, I chose agents with their CRS designation as a target market for
growing my business. Today I am writing because I would like to build an ongoing
business relationship with you and become a part of your referral network. I would
like to know more about you and your real estate business. And likewise I would like
you to know more about me and how I can help increase your opportunities. If you
are not pursuing CRS agent referrals yourself, I encourage you to utilize this target
market as an important part of your business plan. Let's share in the profits to this
market together!

Enclosed you will find information on my background and specializations as well as
referral comments from clients, agents, and my manager. When I refer a valued
client or customer to an agent I know and trust, I feel I am providing the very best
service. But often I do not personally know an agent in an area where I need to send
a referral. The results are missed business opportunities or delayed real estate
services simply because I do not have a reliable real estate resource for a particular
market. By providing you with some background on me, I hope you will feel confident
in calling me for any West Seattle real estate needs you may have. Together we can
provide the highest level of professional real estate service.

I look forward to meeting you and doing business with you. And, I welcome the
opportunity to know more about you and your area of expertise so that I can send
you referrals. Please keep in touch.

Regards,

Mallory Shibuya, CRS
Associate Broker
Windermere Real Estate

want referrals, your motto should be, "Overwhelm the referring agent with communication." If you don't have a written system to confirm the referral, create one now. I suggest when you get the referral you immediately put it in writing. Send a copy for signature to the other agent. Keep a copy for your records. Weekly, call the referring agent with an update.

Get testimonials from ecstatic agents. If you're following my advice, you're going to get enthusiastic comments from your referring agents. Ask them to put those comments in writing. In addition, always send them a survey after closing. Figure 5.3 is a survey you can use. You'll get plenty of material to use as testimonials. Remember, somehow you must make your potential customer (the agent, in this case) comfortable and confident with your service—*before* they actually have an opportunity to experience that service.

Network Marketing: A Concept for the 21st Century

These four sources of business for the experienced agent are generated by a marketing concept called networking: creating business by establishing trustworthy business relationships over time. Getting more business from people who have known you and come to trust you is an old business-producing concept. It's the one my dad taught me as I watched him establish a successful meat market and meat-packing business in a small town. Networking is coming back as *the* most important business-producing method for the 21st century. Why? Marketers in all fields are discovering that the methods of marketing used in the 1970s and 1980s just don't work as well as they used to. The consumer is more sophisticated and is overwhelmed with marketing messages. The mass media advertising that has been so popular in the past has gotten too expensive for the results gained. There isn't adequate return on investment. An example is what's happened with local newspaper advertising. Many real estate companies have decided not to advertise in their newspapers because they do not get adequate results. Some real estate agents are lagging behind in waking up to wasting marketing dollars. They're still chasing strangers in the mass media, just as real estate companies did in the past. In my survey of exceptional agents, several of them mentioned that one of the biggest mistakes agents make is to spend too much money on advertising:

Figure 5.3   Survey to Referring Agent after Closing

So that I can make sure that I'm providing the kind of service that encourages you to refer to me again, please let me know how I did. Thanks for having confidence in me to refer your valued customers.

1. Did I communicate with you promptly to let you know that I had called/met with the client?   yes   no

   If no, how could I have communicated better?

2. Throughout the transaction, how was my communication with you? (on a scale of 1 to 5, with 5 being high) 1 2 3 4 5

   How could I improve my communication?

3. Did the client seem satisfied with my service?   yes   no

   How could I improve my service to the client?

4. Would you feel comfortable referring other clients to me?   yes no

   How could I earn more of your referrals?

5. I hope you were happy with my service. If so, would you please write me a phrase that I can provide to other agents so they'll have confidence in me?

Do I have your permission to use your comments in my brochure? yes   no

Signed: _____

- "I see agents wasting money on marketing techniques that feed only their own ego. I see them marketing to the masses instead of focusing on their past clients and sphere of influence." Julie Davis, owner

- "I see agents marketing in publications to the masses. Billboards, ego advertising throws away thousands of dollars." Karen McKnight, sales associate

- "Too many agents try to buy the business—advertising, mail-outs, giveaways—only to avoid person-to-person contact." Rick Franz, sales associate

Media advertising is not the best way to grow a business. The best marketing strategy going into the twenty-first century is *networking,* which includes all the principles we've been talking about in this chapter. Networking is creating long-term relationships with influential people, who in turn introduce us to more people we can help. That's a key concept for our business. We build trust and confidence not by blaring that we're professional but through our *actions*. However, because the customer doesn't know what he's getting until he *doesn't*, we must have some way to help people choose the *right* agent—before we get into action. That's done through the power of networking . . . people saying nice things about how we work.

Consistency and Frequency Are Key

Consistency and frequency are key to network marketing. The principle of this relationship selling is to follow up until they *buy or die.* Now, if an agent is thinking only short-term, he's not going to be concerned about lifelong marketing. But, if the agent's overall business strategy is to build a steel-girded business foundation for the future, he's going to embrace the three principles of network marketing:

Communicate (1) *consistently* and (2) *frequently* until they (3) *buy or die. Consistently* means at regular intervals. Marketers recommend at least four times yearly, spaced evenly apart. *Frequently* means often enough so that the recipient of your messages remembers who you are. *Buy or die* means, of course, that, you never take them off your mailing list! Have you been using these marketing principles in your business plan?

A New Business Strategy Is Evolving

A different kind of overall business strategy is required. Because the consumer's demands have changed, the old-style short-term-thinking agent is losing ground. We see, too, that it's taking longer to establish a strong real estate business today, because the consumer has grown so wary of salespeople. The good news is that, for the people who want to make a *career* out of the business and are patient about building it correctly, the trends are in their favor:

- Consumers like the idea that agents care about what happens to them over the long term.

- Consumers grasp that it's not in their best interest to be manipulated by fear sales tactics or greed.

- Consumers, confused by the information overload, are seeking advice from those they trust—they're networking.

Julie Davis said it beautifully: "Yesteryear's REALTOR® was the *controller* of information. Today's REALTOR® is the *interpreter* of information. We have arrived at the higher level of professionalism we have desired for so long. With this new level of professionalism comes the need for different skills and a higher level of accountability." Julie's observations are right in line with that higher accountability demanded by our consumer today. Dedicated careerists like you will meet the challenges to create more meaningful long-term customer relationships.

Caring about the sellers and buyers who didn't choose to work with us means that we are looking at our businesses as long-term personal investments. We're looking at buyers and sellers not as instant paychecks, but as business referral sources. And, in order for them to be referral sources, we must do the right thing by them—whether or not we list or sell their homes. Explaining this overall business strategy to your potential buyers or sellers puts a whole different light on your long-term business relationships, and helps sellers and buyers choose you—an agent who really cares about their best interests. So you can hear how this approach sounds, I'm including it role-played on the audiotape.

Summary

We've explored sources of business for the experienced agent that reinforce the notion of network marketing for the twenty-first century. These four sources are

1. sellers who didn't list with you,

2. buyers who didn't buy with you,

3. your former business associates, and

4. other agents.

These four sources are not *primary*. That is, we don't expect them to buy or sell with us immediately. We are networking with them for referrals. This business approach supports the premise that you intend to be a long-term careerist, devoted to helping people throughout their lives in real estate decisions. It's the wave of the future for success in real estate. This approach elevates real estate salespeople from the old-style manipulative sales techniques to true consultants and counselors. It helps keep you focused on delightful customer service. It will dramatically change the way you do your business and your results. Get started with this approach and these sources now.

Your Tune-Up for Chapter 5

✓ Practice your dialogue for sellers; create the survey in Figure 5.1 and use it.

✓ Practice your dialogue for buyers to create referral business.

✓ Read three business books on networking and creating delighted customers for life.

✓ Make a list of 100 people from your former business life.

✓ Make a list of 50 agents who you think will refer to you. Create your version of Mallory's letter in Figure 5.2. Start using the survey in Figure 5.3.

The action plan of calling on these people for referrals will start in your four-week plan. Get prepared now to carry out the plan aggressively and diligently. Remember, consistency and frequency are everything in network marketing. Keep in contact with those you know, consistently and frequently, until they buy or die.

6

Getting into High Gear to Control the Listing Process

I avoid the peaks and valleys of real estate by consistently listing homes that will sell in normal market time.

—Nada Sundermeyer, CRS, GRI, sales associate

Nada was probably referring to *economic* peaks and valleys. In addition, listing homes that *don't* sell sends us agents into *emotional* "valleys of depression." In this chapter, I'll show you how to avoid both the economic and emotional valleys that we experience when we use old-fashioned listing practices. I'll show you how to put new strategies into your listing process so that you have greater control—both economically and emotionally.

Don't List, Don't Last

Most likely, if you've been in the real estate business for over a couple of minutes, you've heard this saying: "If you don't list, you don't last." Many companies and agents are still running their business based on the premise that, to survive, they must have lots of signs in yards. That premise is no longer true. In fact, it's hurting the reputation of companies and agents. Before we explore that idea, let's look at how that premise started.

Historically, real estate companies launched their businesses by hiring agents and sending them out to "get the word out." The best way to advertise a new company in town was to get for sale signs up. That meant "getting listings" was the name of the game. The company with the most listings had the biggest listing market share. The CEO of that company then had bragging rights. You've seen the ads, "We are number one. We have more listings than anyone else." The philosophy was, if the public knew that lots of people listed with that company, more of the public would then list with that company. This whole approach made it sound to agents as if getting listings, not getting them sold, was the objective of a real estate company and its associates.

Getting Listings Works in a Sellers' Market

Sellers' markets support high-pricing strategies for company growth. The company-growth strategy, get listings, worked well as long as it was a "seller's market"—more buyers than sellers, resulting in appreciating home prices. With buyers competing for properties, the listings practically sold themselves. Of course, getting listings doesn't necessarily mean income. For an agent to make money, either

1. the listings must *sell* to result in revenue, or
2. listings must be used as bait and switch to get buyers.

In an appreciating market, these two strategies worked to create revenue. Buyers were buying for fear that the home they wanted would be sold if they didn't make a buying decision quickly. So buyers, anxious to find a home, easily "turned themselves in" to a real estate agent by calling on a sign or ad. The companies and the agents were able to create revenue, one way or the other. The appreciating market covered up several marketing mistakes that the companies and agents were engaging in:

- Enough showings were generated by anxious buyers that the sellers weren't aware their overpriced home was being used as a bait and switch (consumers shouldn't be baited and switched).

- The market was appreciating fast enough to finally come up to meet the sellers' overinflated price—over time (overpricing products is a poor strategy).

- The company and agent's best interests were first, not those of the consumer (consumers should come first).

Sales Skills for a Sellers' Market

A whole set of sales skills was developed for this get listings strategy. Because the objective was not to *sell* the home, only to *list* the home, agents developed a "sales spiel" to convince the sellers that they should list with that particular agent and company. Since agents didn't really care if they got the listing priced right, they didn't develop pricing skills or a pricing presentation. (You'll still hear these old sales spiels today with many experienced agents.) However, it wasn't always peaches and cream. As time went on, and the home didn't sell, the sellers' patience wore out. They wanted to know why their home hadn't sold. To deal with this unpleasant development, the agent developed a second sales spiel. The objective of the agents here was to keep the seller from canceling the listing while the agents waited out the escalation of the market. Usually it worked. The market came up, over time, to meet the listed price. The home sold. Because the agents' objective had been met, they really didn't care how happy the sellers were. After all, the agents had gotten lots of buyers from the signs and ads!

Emerging Buyers' Market Changes All

Buyers' market puts a screeching halt to sellers' market sales strategy. A few years ago, the real estate industry started experiencing longer and deeper "buyers' markets"—depreciating real estate values, more sellers, and fewer buyers. In a buyers' market, the buyers call the shots. They have no competition to purchase the property, so they can negotiate from a power position. As you can imagine, the sellers' market sales strategy artfully employed by agents didn't work in these buyers' markets. Neither did the sales spiels offered by agents to sellers when they became disgruntled when their homes didn't sell. There was no appreciating market to cover the pricing sins of the agents. There were no buyers looking at the home. Agents were getting "egg on their face" because they had secured the listing by bragging how great they and their company were. The result was companies and agents created *low customer satisfaction* ratings. After all, if the consumers' earlier experience in a sellers' market was that they got lots of showings and lots of offers, then why shouldn't it always be that way? And, when the sellers didn't get fast results, the sellers gave the agents—and companies—poor marks on customer service. The "company comes first" marketing strategy wasn't getting the results the companies and agents needed to build business.

If Your Listings Don't *Sell*, You Don't Last

A new motto is needed for the 21st century—and now. I've explained a bit about how that "if you don't list" phenomenon got to be a popular motto in real estate. You're getting the picture of why that motto doesn't work well today. We agents are generally using sellers' market sales strategies to list properties. We're treating sellers as we treated them 20 years ago—telling them what we think they want to hear to get the property listed and worrying about the rest later. Perhaps you think I'm being harsh. I wish I were. What do the statistics tell us about the results of our pricing strategies? In our area, where the market is very good now, only 35 percent of all listed properties sell during a 180-day period! That tells me that the listing philosophy agents are using is "if you don't list, you don't last." Instead, listing agents' motto should be "if your listings don't sell within a reasonable period of time, you don't last."

The Consumer Is in the Driver's Seat

Consumers are the drivers. They're driving to Toledo, but we're giving them a roadmap to Fort Lauderdale. Imagine you and I were to take a trip. You were driving. We had agreed to go to Toledo, Ohio. But, I gave you directions to Fort Lauderdale, Florida. It would take us awhile to figure out what's wrong—and how to get on the right track. While we tried to straighten out the confusion, we could get very irritated with each other!

That's what I see happening to sellers and agents today. The sellers want to get their homes sold. The agents want listings (they're using that old sellers' market sales strategy). So, the agents agree to list the homes at a price that they know won't get a sold sign on the property in a reasonable time. They're giving the sellers a roadmap for a *listing*. But, the sellers expect a *sold sign* on the listing, so they need a roadmap for that.

Some Sellers Are on a Test Drive

What if the seller doesn't want a sold sign? When I talk to agents about the principles in this chapter, they tell me that sometimes they can't list the home at the right price. In some cases, some sellers just want to test the market. So, to be "helpful," the agents say they'll put a sign up as a courtesy to sellers. So, now agents and sellers are at least going to Toledo, right? The sellers want to test the market and the agents don't care if the listings sell. You may say that the sellers aren't hurt. But, what about the company reputation? Is the agents' business hurt or helped by this strategy?

Let's think about all those consumers who see that sign. Ever been to a party where someone comes up to you and asks, "You're with ABC Realty. Why can't your company get my friend's home sold?" Are you going to answer, "Well, Sir, we're not really serious about getting homes sold. Your friend Mr. Seller isn't serious about selling that home. We're just helping Mr. Seller test the market. We put up signs just to try to find some out-of-area buyer who might not know the difference." That sounds professional. . . . I'm sure when "Sir" lists his property, he'll call ABC Realty. Not. The professional image of every agent in that company has just gone down a notch when an agent "sponsors a home" into the multiple listing service.

Any company can list properties. Only a few companies and agents consistently get sold signs on their listed properties. Which would you want when you need to sell your home? What's your professional boundary? Do you want to be known as a "sponsor" or a "listings sold" professional? Your future income is directly tied to the decisions you make about your listing "position." We'll be working more on your approach to the business in Chapter 8, "Building the Value of You."

What's the Agent's Objective?

Agents know that the only way they'll make money from listing that home is if a *sold sign* is put on the listing sign. Why, then, would agents list a home that they weren't sure would sell at the listed price? The reasons agents give me are these:

- I'll get that listing and then "get the seller down in price" (sounds like a wrestling contest, doesn't it?).
- I'll use the home to get sign and ad calls, and then switch the buyers to a better-priced property.

To this agent, his objectives come first. If you didn't know these comments were from agents, what kind of salesperson would you think would be talking like this? Sounds like some used car salespeople to me. We agents certainly don't like to think of ourselves that way. But, here's the disturbing conclusion. Our actions in listing properties indicate that using sellers *for our benefit only* is what's on our minds. If only about one-third of the properties listed sell in half a year, what do you think the public calls agents?

Listing homes for the agent's opportunity to bait and switch results in low customer satisfaction. Earlier, I told you about the Consumer Reports survey that showed there were only three things that resulted in high customer satisfaction levels (a sold sign in a quick time period at close to full price). But, because we so rarely accomplish those three things, we unwittingly create low customer satisfaction levels. We think we're gaining high customer satisfaction levels when we dutifully communicate with sellers and work hard for them. Although those activities are *expected* by sellers, they won't get us high customer satisfaction levels unless we get a sold sign on the property fast, and at close to full price. In the twenty-first century, it's critical to our very survival that we concentrate not on our own needs first, but on the consumer's. The desired chain of events is

1. a well-priced listing results in

2. a sold sign, which results in

3. a satisfied customer, which results in

4. a "success" network, which results in

5. your survival—and greater success!

What's a delighted seller worth to you in future dollars? You're a business person. To optimize your business opportunities, you'll want to think about "return on your investment." What's your listing effort worth now? What's it worth in the future to building your business? Would you rather overprice a property, create a disgruntled seller and find four strangers to buy various properties, or would you rather have a delighted seller who'll tell ten people about how wonderful you are? Which is the best source of business for you? Which is the easiest? Which costs you more money? Which enhances your reputation as a professional?

This idea of "enhancing your reputation as a professional" was brought home to me one day by a buyer I was working with. Pam was the kind of buyer who wants the agent to think that she knows more than the agent! Pam was critical and controlling about every aspect of the home buying process. She was one of my biggest challenges. Naturally, I was curious about the person who listed her and Bill's home in Newport Beach, California. I knew the home had been sold quickly, and for close to full price. From Pam's conversation, it was obvious she respected the real estate agent. I asked her how she found the agent. She told me she was referred to this agent by friends of hers. He was highly recommended for his professionalism. She noticed that this agent (a one-man company) had a large market share in the area, and that the properties sold fast. She called this agent, and they met. Pam, of course, had a price in mind in the next higher range than did the agent (as most sellers do). At Pam's price, the agent said, the home wouldn't sell. Then, the agent told Pam, "As you know, I have the best reputation in this area. I'm known for listing fair-priced properties that sell. Taking one overpriced listing to get another sign is not nearly as important to me as my reputation. I want to work with you, and my objective is the same as yours—a sold sign on your property. You are hiring me as a professional. Let me be one." Pam was so impressed that she and her husband listed the property at the right price, got their money, and were able to purchase a wonderful home in Seattle. How did the agent get the reputation? He earned it through his listing practices. Later in this chapter we'll talk about some strategies throughout the prelisting period to set your posture for professionalism and stay true to your strategy for "sold signs on properties" (if you choose this strategy).

The brakes are off, the car is out of control, and I'm bailing out! For many of us, listing an overpriced property makes us feel like that. We don't want to get in that position, and, when we do, we don't know how to get out. From my experience, it's much better to avoid getting in that position than to develop strategies to manipulate irate sellers. Did I say "easier?" No. It's easier at the beginning to take a listing at any price. Then, it gets really hard. It's more difficult to get a listing priced right at the beginning. But, if it's better for all the parties involved, we owe it to the seller, our company, our fellow agents, and our profession to work hard at listing properties with competence.

Putting it in "first" gear going up so we can coast down the hill. An engine has to get into first gear, work hard to go up a hill, so that it can enjoy coasting down the other side. Like that engine, our hard work should be done *prior* to listing the property. That hard work includes

- asking many questions of the sellers to find out their qualifications, demands, and motivations;
- providing information to the sellers so that they can make the best decision for themselves;
- completing adequate research on market trends, competition, and pricing; and
- creating a marketing plan, including pricing, that answers the needs of the sellers, market, and property.

With these things in place prior to listing the property, it's just a matter of carrying out the plan once the property is on the market. It's very difficult to make changes in a marketing plan, including pricing, after the property has impacted the market. Yes, changes can be made, but the first impression is a lasting one. You and the seller never have as much power as you have *before* you expose the property to the market. Making poor marketing decisions (including pricing) up front takes thousands of dollars out of the sellers' pockets. The bottom line is that you don't want to convince the sellers you want to list their property. You want to find out whether working with those sellers will result in a sold sign on their property. You should be qualifying the sellers more stringently their they are qualifying you.

A marketing process for the twenty-first century. This book is not about the listing process. However, because you want to change the way you do business for better results, I want to show you a sketch of the process that I think works for our savvy consumer today. Figure 6.1 shows the events that should occur *before* the property is listed. The differences between this and older-style marketing processes are the following:

- Much more information is provided early on to the seller.
- Many more questions are asked of the seller, to determine values, motivations, needs, challenges.
- Qualification of the seller and property by the agent occur at each step during the process.
- Educating through prioritizing information is the objective, not "getting a listing."
- Demonstrating professionalism for referrals is the objective, not closing for a listing.
- A "sold listing" is the end objective, not a listing.

Listing Principles for Your Future Success

Compare your listing process with that in Figure 6.1. What's different? Are you using an information-based, questioning process? The following are six principles that will change the way you list properties, and make you much more successful in this business.

Principle One: It's Not What You Say, It's What They Think *about What You Say*

Have you ever heard an agent complain that he or she gave the seller a great market analysis, and the seller listed with someone else at a

Figure 6.1 The Marketing Process for Right-Priced Listings

STEP	PROCESS	ACTIVITIES

1. Have first meeting/ conversation in person or on phone. → Critical qualifying questions asked of seller (if not qualified, don't continue).

↓

Informational material given or sent to qualified seller regarding marketing principles and your professional guidelines (prelist package).

↓

2. First visit: Do research at the home on home and seller (seller at home). → Ask critical qualifying questions and do walk-through (if seller and/or home not qualified, don't continue). Informational material given to seller (first visit package).

↓

3. Create Marketing Plan (including price), prepared at the office.

↓   ↓

4. Second Visit: Present Marketing Plan (given to seller) in person. → Presentation is given with visuals and statistics. If seller is cooperative and the home is priced right, list the property.

Note: This process may occur in one visit or more with the seller. I've described two visits, because most agents develop this process through two visits.
Important: This process should be followed, no matter the time frames.

higher price? We all want to believe good news. We don't want to believe less attractive things. In fact, sometimes we even shoot the messenger. That's actually what sellers do when they choose the agent who gives them the highest price. They "shoot down" all the other agents! But, how do you convince the seller that your price is right? You must

1. provide credibility for your statements *visually* through educating the seller (verifiable statistics, for example), and

2. prove *you're* credible (testimonials).

Now, don't get me wrong. I don't mean merely to provide comparable properties in solds, on the markets, and expireds. I mean to educate the seller about how the market works:

1. The trends of the market (going up, going down, availability of sellers, buyers)

2. Buyer habits today (how many homes looked at, list price ratio to buying price, etc.)

3. Best marketing strategies for this market—and why, with statistics to back up your claims

Principle Two: Six Times Is the Charm

Do you know how many times we must hear and see something to remember it? Six times. How many times do we actually attempt to teach sellers the principles we've been discussing? What do we have to reteach? What perceptions of sellers do we have to change in order to be effective? So, principle two means that you must take all the major, important principles you need to teach sellers and package them to appear *six times* during your prelisting communication. Let's take one principle as an example: Overpricing costs the seller money. Here's how that principle can be shown to a seller six times:

1. In your prelisting package that you drop off to sellers right after you meet them, put a letter in your packet from a seller whose listing expired, and who then listed with you (and the home sold fast).

2. In the prelisting package, state your listing philosophy and why it's good for everyone. Include letters from sellers you've helped with your philosophy.

3. In your first visit to the home, as you're walking through gathering research on the home, observe that several properties in the area have been on the market for a long time, while others have sales on them. Be specific, using a particular property in that area.

4. During your seller interview in the first visit, while you're gathering information from the sellers (your seller research), ask the sellers how long they intend to let their home stay on the market without a sale; when would they become dissatisfied with the level of service by their listing agent when the home doesn't get a sale; why would they imagine one home would get an offer, while another in the same area and general price range wouldn't? Ask the sellers, "What would cause you to enthusiastically refer me to others?" "What would cause you to avoid referring me?"

5. In your first-visit packet of materials, leave information about homes that were listed at market value and the kind of activity they enjoyed (number of showings, offers, bidding, sale prices, versus homes that "begged" for offers and the results).

6. In your marketing presentation, tell the seller that the promotional plan (all those activities you'll do after listing) is not effective with the wrong price. For example, "Mr. Seller, I will hold a broker's open house for you. It's very important, wouldn't you agree, that we make our first impression a very favorable one. We want the agents to be so excited about your home that they'll immediately make appointments with their buyers. In fact, we want this home to be so attractive in all ways that several buyers will try to buy this home at once. Wouldn't that get you a better price and a more pleasant selling experience!"

Principle Three: You're a **Marketer,** *Not Just a* **Pricer**

Have you been in a store when someone was "marking the inventory"—that is, putting prices on it? That's a "pricer." If you tell a seller that you'll present a "market analysis" on their property, they think you're merely a "marker"—a pricer. To be a professional, you must be so much more than that. The right job description for you is "marketer." What does that mean? That means you understand and use the marketing process to sell properties. Here's that process:

1. Research all aspects of the marketing problem (research the market trends, the market area, the subject property, and the seller).

2. Gather and analyze all research to come to marketing conclusions.

3. Create and present a marketing plan to the seller. The marketing plan includes the *research, conclusions of the research, promotional strategies of the company, office, and you, and pricing.*

4. Implement the promotional part of the plan as the listing period starts. Measure the results.

Marketing is not just pricing. It's not just promotion. It's the whole process. We agents have unwittingly devalued ourselves in doing market analyses instead of marketing *plans*. In today's world, we agents must think in terms of the whole plan and communicate that concept to sellers.

Principle Four: Anticipate the Objections

In old-style selling, agents were taught to try to close someone and then wait for the objections. Then, agents were taught how to "counter" the objections. Now, I'm not saying that learning to deal with objections is bad. It's not. It's good. What I'm saying is that closing and waiting for people to push back on the agent is, in itself, old-style manipulative sales. Instead, the smart real estate marketers of today put together their marketing plans today based on the information they learned during their research period. Remember, that research includes the information the seller gave them during the seller interview. That information included sellers' viewpoints about

- reasons for selling (motivation of all sellers),
- what will happen if the sellers can't sell within a certain period of time,
- other agents they're talking to,
- good/bad agent experiences they've had,
- criteria they'll use to pick an agent, and
- marketing strategies they think are good.

Do you have these areas covered in your seller interview? Are you doing a seller interview now? When do you do it during the marketing process? What are you learning from it? How are you using the information you're gathering in the seller interview?

By asking questions early on in this marketing process to reveal a seller's perceptions, you can then create a marketing strategy that answers these questions and changes the seller's perceptions. Here's a critical point. When you ask these questions, do not argue. Do not "answer objections." You're just gathering information. Either say "thank you for your opinion," or probe with "tell me more about that." I'll role play this interview process on the audiotape. One of the biggest mistakes agents make is that they do not gather enough information from the seller early on to create a good marketing plan for that seller. Then, they fail to list the property because they didn't present a plan that created confidence in the agent and that changed the seller's perceptions.

After gathering all the information from the seller, put together a marketing plan with statistics, testimonials, and other visuals that prove your marketing approach. Then, you won't have to verbally wrestle with the seller when it comes to price. You'll have taught the seller the important marketing concepts both of you must understand and use to get a sold sign on his property.

Principle Five: You Are Now Teacher, Information Analyzer and Prioritizer, Counselor, Marketer, and Business Partner

To succeed in the future, you can no longer be merely in sales, although you must also be a terrific salesperson. To work with the sophisticated consumer of today, you must be able to

- *analyze* market and seller information,
- *facilitate* open discussion with sellers to introduce new concepts,
- *prioritize* information in a systematized, logical format,
- *communicate* this prioritized information to the seller,
- *teach* the seller today's marketing concepts,
- *counsel* with the seller to maintain positive relationships, and
- *partner* with the seller to reach mutual objectives.

Looking at that list, what skills do you already have that you can apply to this different approach? What skills do you need? How will you get them? Several of these skills are management and teaching skills. One way you can grasp these new skills is through taking "CRB" courses. The Managers' Council of the National Association of Realtors presents a series of managers' courses nationally that address these areas. These courses are called "CRB" courses because they lead to the CRB designation. "CRB" stands for "certified real estate broker." Call 1-800-323-0248 for information about courses in your area. (The CRB and CRS abbreviations are explained in the References section.)

Principle Six: Making One Customer Delighted (Through the Sale of His or Her Home) Begets You More Customers at Less Cost

In the coming years, agents and companies must concentrate on the customers they have—and had—for more business. That doesn't mean waiting for a seller to sell again. That means providing such stunning service and keeping in touch so well that a seller will refer ten sellers and buyers in five years. How much does this cost you? Much less than ads cost. What kind of business does referral business provide you? Much more pleasant business than working with distrusting strangers.

Tuning Up Your Listing Approach

Now it's time to look at your entire listing process. Using the analysis tool in Figure 6.2, rate yourself on your process from beginning to end. Using the principles in this chapter, refine your listing approach until you become a "pro" for the twenty-first century.

Are These Sellers Qualified to Work with You?

Time management is the agent's biggest challenge. Those time management challenges generally come from an agent's prioritizing his or her real estate activities—wrongly. One of the most common time binds agents get into occurs when they list an overpriced home. Then, they spend all their time in promotional activities to convince other agents and buyers that the home isn't really overpriced! Of course, that doesn't work, and the agents have just invested too much time and money in a project that won't pay off in dollars. Worse yet, the agents will never get referrals from the seller.

To avoid this situation, I've created a checklist for you to use right after you've researched the home and the seller. Before you sign your name on that listing, and commit yourself to many long hours and lots of marketing money, take the time to complete this checklist (Figure 6.3). Completing it will tell you whether that seller deserves your time, attention, and expertise. You're doing just like all other professionals do: You're qualifying that potential client to be able to work with you. Doctors, accountants, and attorneys all turn down clients. As a professional who treasures your reputation, you must, too.

Figure 6.2 How Professional Is Your Listing Process?

Below are the specific activities, systems, and processes that successful agents (20+ units listed and sold per year) perform to consistently list and sell 90% of their listed properties.

FIRST VISIT OR FIRST PART OF THE VISIT   YES   NO

1. Prior to first visit, you ask five critical qualifying questions on the phone to determine that this is a bona fide listing appointment. ☐ ☐
2. You go to only bona fide listing appointments. ☐ ☐
3. You use a checklist to inspect their home with them and record the inspection. ☐ ☐
4. You use a written list of the ten critical "seller qualifying" questions and note the answers in writing. ☐ ☐
5. You give the sellers a packet of information that includes information about the company, the process, and YOU. ☐ ☐
6. The information about you shows your specialties and includes testimonials. It addresses anticipated seller objections. ☐ ☐

RESEARCH AND SECOND VISITS

1. You use a method to design a specific marketing presentation for each of your sellers based on the information you got from the sellers on the first visit. ☐ ☐
2. Your marketing presentation consists of two *equal* parts:
   (i)   The promotions you'll do (Marketing System)
   (ii) The pricing you suggest ☐ ☐
3. You use visual presentations for each of the two parts:
   (i)   A promotional portfolio ☐ ☐
   (ii) A pricing portfolio ☐ ☐
4. Your promotional portfolio shows at least ten special promotional tactics your company and office uses to get the seller's home sold. ☐ ☐
5. Your promotional portfolio shows at least five *special* promotional tactics you personally will do to sell that home. ☐ ☐
6. You have at least 15 pieces of evidence to anticipate and defuse sellers' 15 most common objections to listing with you at your price and commission. ☐ ☐
7. At least half of your promotional portfolio consists of your specific marketing strategies. ☐ ☐
8. You use a marketing calendar to show sellers when your marketing events will occur. ☐ ☐
9. You give sellers their own special marketing plan—and ask them to approve it. ☐ ☐
10. You use your promotional visuals to remind sellers that all those promotions work *only* when the pricing is right. ☐ ☐
11. You have at least three visuals to show how listing at a lower commission assures the listing will sell at longer market time and lower price. ☐ ☐
12. You have at least three visuals to show how taking your recommendations gets houses sold—at top price—and fast. ☐ ☐
13. You have at least three visuals to show why listing at a higher price than your recommendations destroys your professional image while it hurts the marketability of the property. ☐ ☐
14. You review pricing *after* you review your promotional strategies. ☐ ☐
15. You use a written agreement of pricing, price reduction, and time frames that you have sellers sign when they list with you at a higher price than your recommendations. ☐ ☐

Scoring: If you checked "yes" 18–21 times, congratulations. You're using the strategies that top agents have proven will work. If you checked "yes" 12–15 times, you're on your way to becoming a high performing listing agent who provides sellers what they want—a "sold" sign on their property. If you checked "yes" less than 12 times, use this checklist to sharpen your listing process, so more sellers, satisfied with your service, will happily recommend you to others.

Figure 6.3 Evaluate Property Salability

1. Property listed at competitive price. Yes_____ No_____

2. Full-term listing agreement. Yes_____ No_____

3. Seller to complete obvious repairs/cleaning prior to showing. Yes_____ No_____

4. Easy access for showing. Yes_____ No_____

5. Yard sign. Yes_____ No_____

6. Immediate possession. Yes_____ No_____

7. Extras included (e.g., appliances). Yes_____ No_____

8. Available for first REALTOR® tour. Yes_____ No_____

9. Government financing terms available.* Yes_____ No_____

10. Owner financing available.* Yes_____ No_____

11. Below-market down payment.* Yes_____ No_____

12. Below-market interest rate.* Yes_____ No_____

13. Postdated price reduction (if needed). Yes_____ No_____

14. Competitive commission. Yes_____ No_____

15. In my evaluation, this property will sell within listed market range, in normal market time for this area. Yes_____ No_____

16. My credibility as a professional will be enhanced by listing this property. Yes_____ No_____

*If market conditions indicate need.

Summary

It's a different, more demanding real estate world out there, one where you'll find the following:

- The consumer demands a higher level of service.
- Consumers will rate you high in customer satisfaction only if you sell their homes fast, at close to full price.
- "If you don't list, you don't last" must be replaced with "If your listings don't sell within a reasonable period of time at close to first list price, you don't last."
- Instead of building your business by using "bait and switch" tactics on sellers, you must build your business with satisfied sellers.
- You must build your business with the relationships you already have; it's less costly and more pleasant.
- Agents must stop arguing with sellers and create presentations that educate and anticipate objections.
- Develop new skills to facilitate, inform, educate, and prioritize.

Through changing your listing practices, you're on your way to long-term success.

Your Tune-Up for Chapter 6

✓ Review the questions you're asking during the research phase of your listing process. Review the objections you've been getting from sellers that you can't answer during the entire process. What questions do you need to create during that initial research phase to build a marketing plan that anticipates objections? (Listen to the audiotape for ideas on this concept.)

✓ Using the three most common objections or roadblocks you've been facing, build a six-time impact throughout your presentation process for each of the objections (as I did in this chapter).

✓ Using the listing process questionnaire (Figure 6.2), go back and refine each part of your presentation process. Ask five successful listing agents for their consultation during this project.

✓ Review the seller qualification checklist (Figure 6.3). Apply it to the last three listings you've gotten that didn't sell. If you had to do it over again, what would you have needed to learn from the seller to protect yourself from this situation? Would you have listed that property? Under what conditions?

✓ Ask two successful listing agents to allow you to accompany them on first and second listing visits. Ask them to accompany you on your first and second visits. Get evaluations from each after the process. Make the changes they suggest and try your presentation again.

7

Shifting Out of "Stall": Getting into Control with Buyers

Know what it is you want and how you plan to get it. Believe and buy into your goals. Review them daily and persist in never giving up till you've gotten where you want to go. Surround yourself with people who are only positive influences along the way.

—Rick Franz, sales associate

This chapter is about working effectively with buyers. I started the chapter with Rick's quote, because I thought it could certainly apply to us in this context. When we choose buyers who become positive influences in our sales careers, we're assuring that we build a business that's both monetarily and emotionally rewarding.

Frequently, though, this isn't the case. From my own sales experience, and from observing others, I've found that buyers can become an emotional as well as financial drain. We can waste precious hours in working with buyers who won't purchase from us. We can ruin our confidence if we work with buyers who won't be loyal. Agents are not prepared, generally, to work with buyers. In my opinion, our industry doesn't provide adequate training at all in this area. The challenges of working with today's consumers are vastly underrated by both companies and agents. So, it's easy for agents to fall into traps while they *think* they're selling someone a home.

In this chapter, I'll be asking you to review your experiences with buyers. How have you chosen and qualified them? What do you want from them? What are the challenges you've faced with them? After we review your past sales approach, I'll introduce some processes to assure that you're getting what you want and deserve from buyers, so that you meet your goals and protect your most important sales asset, your self-esteem. Putting the strategies in this chapter into your "buyer work" will put the *fun* back into your sales career.

Buyers Can Present a Time Management Challenge

How many potential buyers a week are you meeting as you prospect? If you've been meeting any less than 50 potential buyers a week, you've doomed yourself to fail in working with buyers. What do I mean? You're not finding enough good potential buyers to be *choosy*. Many agents' first mistake in working with buyers is that they work with *anyone* who says he or she is a buyer. Many agents believe that the objective of the sales game is to get someone to put in your car—anyone. So, they prospect only until they find a warm body who wants to look at homes. Then, they try awfully hard to sell this body something. Their time management flies out the window, because they're spending too much time trying to sell something to someone who just won't say yes. When the salespeople can't get the buyer to a "yes," salespeople are stumped. So, they read books and attend sales skill courses to find out how to close the unwilling buyer. Give it up. No one can. You can't. I can't. Why?

The buyer doesn't want to buy! Successfully working with buyers starts with having *too many to choose from!* Let's say you're prospecting faithfully. You're meeting dozens of potential buyers. Now, you've got an enviable problem. You can't put them all in your car, or you'd be dragging them—and you—all over town day and night! Actually, that's not a bad problem to have, though, is it? Wouldn't you rather have too many prospects and have to take time out to qualify them, than to have only one prospect and feel you must work with that prospect to have something to do?

What the Buyer Wants and What the Agent Wants May Be Two Different Things

As a new agent, my husband Dick thought that only serious buyers would want to look at homes. He met an older couple at an open house. They told him they wanted to relocate from West Seattle to Bellevue, about a half-hour drive away. Because they told Dick they didn't drive, Dick drove over to West Seattle, picked them up, and showed them homes in Bellevue. This went on for weeks. Interestingly, this couple always wanted Dick to pick them up about 11 A.M. Then, around noon, they'd ask Dick to take them to lunch. Although they looked at dozens of homes, Dick never could find a home they liked. The last straw was when they asked Dick how much money he intended to spend on their housewarming present—should they buy from him. Dick pulled the car to the side of the road and asked them if they intended to buy—and if they intended to buy from him. They said "no"—twice! Lucky for them Dick didn't just leave them out in suburbia! Why do people want to spend their precious time looking at homes if they don't intend to buy? My observations are that "looky-loos" may

- want to get out of the house,
- look at pretty homes for decorating ideas, or
- get lunch from an agent.

Of course, an agent doesn't want to waste time working with those who have something different in mind than purchasing a home. However, if we don't learn to ask certain insightful questions, we can find ourselves as tour guides—and hosts, as Dick did.

How to Avoid Wasting Your Time with Nonbuyers

First, I've got to admit to you that, as a new agent, I put almost everyone and anyone in my car. No one told me or taught me to qualify. So, I simply showed homes to anyone who wanted to see them. I showed homes six or eight times a week for my first year in the business! In doing so, I did learn several things (besides exhausting myself). I learned the inventory. I learned how to find my way around our large market area. The most important lesson I learned was that, just because people express an interest in looking at homes, they are not necessarily ready, willing, and able buyers. At first, when I realized people were using me for their own purposes, I was mad and hurt. Then, I decided if I was naive enough to be their tour guide, shame on me. To get control of the situation, I created strategies to find out *up front*

- *whether* this person intended to buy,
- *if* this person could buy,
- *when* this person intended to buy, and
- if this person intended to *buy from me.*

Finding the answers to these questions is, of course, called "qualifying." All professionals qualify. It's the same process you go through when you go to the doctor's office. The doctor won't treat you until you fill out forms. The doctor wants to find out certain things to figure out whether he can help you—and how. You'd be really scared if, when you went into the doctor's office, the doctor *didn't* hand you a form to fill out! Unfortunately, few agents have a qualifying process that proves they are as professional as a doctor. Yet, agents are advising buyers about very important decisions—decisions that could affect their lives as much as the advice of a doctor.

Key questions in the qualifying process. Agents need to know the answers to questions that begin with those prepositions you learned in grade school: *Who, what, when, where, how.*

In each of these categories, here are key questions that will tell you whether your buyer is qualified to work with you:

- *What*—What will a different home accomplish for you? You must find out what buyers' motivations are for purchasing. (Insufficient motivation means they won't buy even if you find them their "dream home.") Agents usually think of "what" questions as "what features do you want in a home." This is not a qualifying question. Be wary of asking the buyers to describe every nook and cranny they want in a home. Unwittingly, you can be encouraging buyers to create in their minds a home that their pocketbooks can't purchase. The important point here is that buyers don't buy homes for the *features* they have. They buy homes for the *emotional needs* these homes fulfill. "*What*" questions should be aimed at finding out emotional needs.
- *When*—When do you intend to purchase?
- *Why*—Avoid using this word. It's confronting. Instead, frame the question as a "what" question.
- *Where*—Find out about all areas they are interested in, including areas you may be not able to show. Do you need to refer them to another agent? Do they have another agent?
- *How*—How will they get the down payment? Do they have a home to sell? How will they start their home search? Do they have an agent? How will they choose an agent?

Compare your questionnaire.   Get out the questionnaire you're now using. Ask yourself:

- What does the questionnaire you're using now consist of?
- How many "feature" questions are on your questionnaire?
- How many insightful questions are there?
- How much time are you taking to get to know your potential customers?
- How many total questions are you asking?
- How many probing questions are you asking to follow up and clarify?
- What do you do with the information you're gathering?
- What has baffled you about your prior buyers that a better question-naire could have uncovered?

A test-marketed, proven process.   Figure 7.1 is a questionnaire that the agents in my office and I have developed to gather the information needed for success in this part of the buyer-counseling process. It will help you uncover the "secrets" that buyers like to keep from agents. It goes further than merely "features" and is arranged in a manner that creates a comfortable rapport-building atmosphere.

Deciding whether to work with the buyer.   It's just as important for your time management to decide who you *won't* work with as to decide who to work with. Looking at the questions on your and my question-naires, what answers would cause you to decide *not* to work with that potential customer? When you draw the line, you start on your road to greater professionalism, time management, and enhanced self-esteem. I've provided a checklist for you, Figure 7.2, which you can use to determine whether your potential client is qualified enough to get to work with you.

Capturing and Keeping the Customers You Want

In this section, I'll show you several strategies you can put to use to have greater control with your buyer. Competition continues to heat up among agents for qualified buyers. To win, agents must get better at being perceived as "exceptional." We must *give the buyer a reason to choose us.*

Figure 7.1   Home Information Form

Exchanging this information prior to seeing properties helps assure you find exactly the right property. In addition to relating the physical requirements you want in your desired home, this questionnaire will help clarify what's really important to you—your lifestyle and values that impact the home you want to purchase.

FAMILY INFORMATION

Name _____ Date _____ Source _____

Address _____ Phone _____ Office Phone _____

No. in family _____ Children _____

    Name _____ Age _____

    Name _____ Age _____

    Name _____ Age _____

Husband's employer _____ Wife's employer _____

Reason for moving _____

Leisure/Interests _____

Will someone else be helping you make your purchase decision?_____

If so, who? _____

LOCATIONS

Preferred school districts _____

Preferred areas—describe feeling/look of area _____

_____

Homes seen in area that you liked _____

What kept you from purchasing? _____

Previous work with agent? When? _____

TIME FRAME

How long have you been looking? _____

What's the reason you haven't purchased? _____

Desired date of possession_____ If we found a home now, could you purchase?_____

HOME FEATURES

____Resale   ____New   ____Bedrooms   ____Baths

____Family room/describe how used _____

____Rec room/describe how used _____

____Basement/describe how used _____

____Kitchen eating space _____ Hardwood floors _____

____Fireplace locations: _____

____Garage/workshop. Describe _____

____Place for hobbies. Describe _____

____Boat parking/storage-function: _____

____Storage/describe _____

____Other considerations/use of: _____

Figure 7.1 Home Information Form - *continued*

HOME STYLE
_____ 2 Story _____ Multi-Level _____ Other
_____ Split _____ Tri-Level
_____ Rambler _____ Daylight Rambler
Why is this style important? _____
_____

HOME SETTING
_____Acreage/function: _____
_____Privacy/explain: _____
_____Trees   Open/sunny_____Garden _____
_____Neighborhood   Describe: _____
Other considerations: _____
_____
Overall home/setting feeling: _____
_____
Moving will accomplish: _____
_____

PRESENT HOME
Do you need to sell your home to buy? _____
What do you like the best: _____
The least: _____
Is your home presently listed for sale? _____
Would you prefer selling your home prior to buying? _____
How did you find your last home? _____
_____
Services you found valuable that an agent provided: _____
_____
How much equity?_____Market analysis needed: _____
Other origins of down payment: _____

FUTURE INVESTMENT
_____ Price _____ Initial Investment
_____ House Payment _____ Terms
Do you know what you qualify for? _____

Figure 7.2　Evaluate Your Customer's Potential

After the first interview, evaluate whether your potential customer is qualified enough to work with you.

Rate on a scale of 1 – 4 (4 being the highest).

	1	2	3	4
1. Customer is motivated to purchase. (Rate each spouse/partner separately)	1	2	3	4
2. Customer is realistic about price range expectations.	1	2	3	4
3. Customer is open and cooperative.	1	2	3	4
4. Customer will purchase in a timely manner.	1	2	3	4
5. Customer is a referral source and will provide referrals.	1	2	3	4
6. The customer has agreed that you will be his or her exclusive agent.	1	2	3	4
7. Agent has established a positive rapport with customer.	1	2	3	4
8. Customer will meet with loan officer.	1	2	3	4
9. Customer answered financial questions openly.	1	2	3	4
10. Customer has no other agent obligations.	1	2	3	4
11. If customer has home to sell, he or she is realistic about price.	1	2	3	4
12. Customer will devote sufficient time to purchasing process.	1	2	3	4
13. Both spouses/partners will be available to look for home.	1	2	3	4

Is this customer worthy of your time, energy, and expertise?

What's Your Procedure with Potential Clients?

Remember that saying, "You never have a second chance to make a first impression." It's proven that people make their minds up about us within the first few seconds of meeting us. Today, potential buyers are talking to more than one agent before making a choice. This is a growing trend. So, it's more important than ever to *differentiate* yourself from other agents immediately upon meeting this potential customer. Agents frequently miss this point. They expect a buyer to find out they're different from other agents when the buyer works with the customer. Sorry, it's too late. If you don't figure out ways to differentiate yourself within the first few minutes of meeting that potential customer, you've lost.

Do You Project the Same Image as Other Agents?

What are the public's assumptions about real estate agents? They think all agents are pretty much the same—and they aren't very satisfied with our level of service. Because they think we make much more money than the average American, the public believes that we should work harder at doing a good job for them than we do. (According to a survey by the National Association of REALTORS®, the public thinks agents make, on average, $50,000 a year. In fact, agents make, on average, about $24,000 yearly!) Armed with the knowledge of what the public thinks of agents, you'll agree that, to be respected and trusted by buyers, you'll need to prove yourself different from their general perceptions. Notice I'm saying *different*. I don't mean you have to brag you're better than other agents, or that you're "number one." That's so passe—and so ineffective. Rather, you have to create strategies that communicate to the potential client that

- you're *different* from their perception of a real estate agent,
- you're worthy of their *trust*,
- your *service* is different than they've encountered or heard about before, and
- you'll keep *their best interest* in mind above your self-interest.

The Challenge of Creating Differentiation

You must prove yourself different from the "average" agent to capture loyalty, trust, confidence, and long-term business from buyers. But, in this age of overcommunication, that's easier said than done. Consumers are getting so much information about *everything* that they just don't have the time or energy to prioritize it. When you go home at night and sort your mail, how much is junk mail? Do you open every piece, sort it into piles of charge card inquiries, charity inquiries, etc.? Do you read every one of those and prioritize them? Do you keep a file over time on each category? Probably none of the above. You toss them in the round file, unopened, unless you have an immediate need.

The public feels the same way about all the information they get from real estate agents. Much of that information is confusing and misleading. The more confusing and misleading the messages, the more the public resists making any decisions. It's human nature. When overwhelmed with information, we just ignore all of it. Do you think this trend of overwhelming communication will continue? Will it get worse? We now have the ability to get more information than we need. We real estate licensees will have an ever-increasing challenge to break through this overwhelming barrage of communication to differentiate ourselves and capture buyers' loyalty.

To prepare for differentiation you must find out what your competition is doing.   What's the level of your competition? What are they saying and doing to differentiate themselves? How good do you have to be to beat it? One of the agents in my office, Martha, found out the other day that you can't beat the competition unless you

- know what they're saying—about themselves and about you,
- have prepared your differentiation materials and script in advance, and
- have presented your differentiations early in the relationship.

Joan, an agent in our office, knocked on doors near her new listing. When she found a potential seller, she invited Martha to work with her, because Martha had been in the business six months longer than Joan and had a strong presentation. Together, they went to the sellers' home to do their research. During this time, they found out that the seller had already made a loose commitment to list with another agent. But, because Martha and Joan were so professional, the sellers decided to put off listing with the other agent for a few days.

However, the sellers told the other agent about Martha and Joan. Knowing he had to differentiate himself from Martha and Joan, the other agent gave questions to the sellers to ask Martha and Joan. Those questions, of course, made the other agent look good and reflected less well on Martha and Joan. One of the questions was, "How long have you been in the business?" Martha and Joan have been selling real estate just over a year. The other agent has been selling for seven years. However,

Martha completed 37 transactions her first year, and Joan completed ten. That's great for first-year agents. The other agent, in contrast, completed 20 in his *seventh* year. Also, from having worked with the other agent, I know that the other agent is not nearly as ethical and Martha and Joan. He makes more enemies than friends, both with customers and agents. He's a smart competitor, though, and he created questions for sellers to ask that would make him look better than the other agents. Even though Martha and Joan answered the questions, they didn't have proof of their sales excellence. After answering the question, they provided proof to the seller. It was too little, too late. They just couldn't get into a controlling position in the interview process.

The good news is that, even though the other agent listed the home, it's listed overpriced and isn't selling. Guess what will happen when the listing expires? Do you think the other agent will receive referrals from the seller? I imagine that Martha and Joan will list the property at the right price, get it sold, and get referrals. It's unfortunate, though, that they didn't have the differentiation ammunition prepared when they first met the seller to create a better first impression.

Three Strategies to Differentiate Yourself

Your objectives when you first meet the potential buyer are to give the customers:

- a reason to *choose* you from all the others, and
- reasons to *trust* you more than the others.

The following are three strong strategies to assure you get what you want.

Strategy One: Let Your Professionalism Precede You

How could you communicate your high professional process even before you've had a chance to show these potential buyers this process? Why not package some information for buyers that demonstrates how you work? Smart listing agents are doing this now for sellers. They call this a prelisting package. Savvy buyers' agents are doing the same thing for potential buyers. Before you decide what to include, ask yourself:

- What are going to be the biggest objections of these buyers to working with me? Anticipate these objections in your package.

- In my area, what do I need to prove I'm different *from*? Put that information in the package.
- What might another competing agent say about me that I want to present positively to these buyers?
- What do I want the buyers to know about prior to my sitting down with them?
- What do I want the buyers to prepare for me prior to my sitting down with them?
- What information about changes—in the market, in how agents work, in the industry, etc., do the buyers need to know about to make a good decision?

With this package, you're becoming a consultant, instead of merely a salesperson. You're gathering and prioritizing information to make it easy for buyers. It's important that you provide this information to buyers early on in the qualifying process. You'll find you'll earn respect and trust. You'll find it much easier to ask—and get—their loyalty. You're also proving that you are one of the few agents who has spent time, expertise, and money to gather and prioritize the information you think buyers need to make a good decision. You'll stand out simply because you took the effort!

Strategy Two: Don't Brag. Let Others Brag about You

We don't believe what we *hear*. We believe what we *see*. Think back for a minute. How did you choose your doctor? Your accountant? You probably asked your friends for referrals. If they gave good "testimony," you felt comfortable calling that professional. Do the same for your potential customer. Let him gain confidence in you by letting *others* brag about you. Use testimonials. How do you get them? One of the ways is to send out surveys at closing. (My book, *The Real Estate Agent's Business Planning Guide*, has a survey you can use.) Also, on the audiotape with this series, I'll role-play some dialogues for you to use in asking for testimonials. Put your testimonials in your pre-list package. Or, develop a Professional Portfolio and put your testimonials there. Of course, if you develop a Portfolio, be sure to give it to the potential buyer very early on in the process. It should be delivered to the buyer at the same time you give the buyer the "prelist package." (Information on creating an effective Portfolio is in the References section of this book.) Remember, your objective in providing "what others say about you" is to raise the respect and trust levels the potential customer has with you.

Strategy Three: Point Out Differentiators

Recently, one of the agents in my office and I were discussing a letter that I received from some sellers we represented. We send surveys at closing to find out how we did and how we can improve. These two sellers, two sisters, took the time to write me a two-page letter in addition to the survey they returned to us. The survey had many nice things to say about the agent and our office.

The letter, though, had areas where, according to the sisters, they felt we could improve. There were several times when the escrow company, agent's assistant, and buyer's agent disappointed the sellers. The sellers felt our agent could have controlled these other parties (which I don't believe we could have). I discussed the letter with the listing agent. She told me that the sellers were under great stress, selling their mother's home. They weren't communicating well together and had a tough time "hearing" things correctly. So, the agent put everything in writing and asked continually of both sisters how to best communicate. Still, the sisters' expectations weren't met.

There were even some heroic behaviors from all the professionals involved. The escrow agent went to the mother's retirement home to get the closing papers signed—at the mother's and sisters' convenience (very unusual these days). Unfortunately, the sisters seemed not to realize that these heroic behaviors were indeed out-of-the-ordinary. Since the sellers hadn't been told that these were indeed heroic behaviors, they thought that these behaviors were ordinary—things done by all escrow agents and listing agents. Then, when they found fault with some of the parties, they concluded that their transaction hadn't been handled well. Doing a better job in promoting these heroic behaviors as differentiators may have resulted in a better overall customer service rating from the sisters.

"Customers don't know what they're getting—until they don't." You must lead your potential customer through the differentiation process. *They* can't differentiate between an expected service and a heroic one if they don't know what's heroic. If you create a strategy for pointing out differentiations, customers will know what they're getting, and hopefully, will appreciate the special things you're doing for them.

Introduce differentiators in your dialogue. Use "differentiation dialogue" to point out areas where you're different from other agents. Here's an example of how to use this dialogue to introduce your prelist package:

Here's a compilation of information I've created for you to help you through the purchasing process. Have you ever seen one of these? I think I'm one of the first agents in the area to create a package to inform potential purchasers. Although it's a lot of work, buyers tell me it's really helped them. With all the confusing information about buying a home today, I wanted to take the time to put together a package that would help you prioritize your concerns. This will save you time and ensure that you get the kind of service you expect—and the kind of home-buying experience you want.

It's not what you do, it's how you promote it. Many agents do wonderful things for buyers and sellers. However, they're "secret agents." They don't let buyers and sellers know that these things are out-of-the-ordinary. So, the customer thinks everyone does these things. It's not enough today to merely tell and show potential buyers (and sellers) what you'll do. You must differentiate yourself by *pointing out the exceptional nature of that service*. This adds value to your service. That's a huge buzz word today, *value-added service*. Get in the habit of developing "differentiation dialogue."

How's your buyer presentation? If you're going to represent buyers, you need a "buyer presentation." This is a well-thought-out process that takes buyers through the buying process, explaining both the process and how you assist. Do you have a visual presentation now? If not, why not? With commissions now being split between buyers and sellers, it's ever more important to formalize the work we do with buyers. But, it's not the information itself that's important. It's that your approach gives messages to the buyers' subconscious. In return, in the back of their minds, you want the purchasers to be saying to themselves, "She's really a 'pro.' Look at how this information is packaged and prioritized for us. She's spent lots of time and money to help us get information easily. She must really be committed to this business. I guess we can trust her."

Figure 7.3 is a list of the materials that can go into a buyer's presentation. A caveat: Never *give* your presentation to buyers to take with them. If you want to leave something with a buyer when you first meet them (at an open house), give them your personal brochure. The presentation I'm referring to here must be "interactive," just like your sellers' marketing presentation. I suggest that you show potential buyers your presentation during the first meeting. You explain that this is the process you and they will do to assure that they get all the information they need to make the best decision for them in today's market.

Figure 7.3 What to Put in Your Buyer's Presentation

Basic Package:
Home Information Form (Figure 7.1)
Agency Brochure/Explanation
Purchase and Sale Agreements
Examples of Loan Programs/Closing Costs
Your Personal Brochure/Promotional Material

Package May Also Contain:
Articles on Market Conditions/Market Statistics
Brochures on Purchasing a Home
Your Newsletter
How Tax Bracket Affects Interest Rates
Area Information (including pertinent maps)
Schools, Utilities, Amenities Information
Financial Information (rates sheets, explanations)
Charts for Escrow Fees
Private Mortgage Insurance Information
Title Insurance Tables

Much of this information is available in brochures from banks, escrow firms, and title companies.

Becoming a Life-Long Partner with Your Customers

An agent came into my office upset because he thought another agent in our office was stealing his customer. I asked him if he had a signed buyer agency agreement with this customer. He told me "no." I asked him if he had gotten a commitment from this customer to be loyal. He said "no." I asked him whose customer, then, it was. He told me, because he'd been *working* with this customer, he thought the customer was his. However, he said, agents in other companies were also showing homes to this customer. He wanted me to protect him from losing the customer to someone else in the office. However, he had taken no steps himself to assure that he *had a loyal client*.

I asked him, if he had no buyers' agency agreement, and he hadn't asked for loyalty, how did he think he had a chance of selling this customer a home? He said, "By showing the customer homes, I'm trying to prove my worth, so the customer will be loyal and buy from me." What do you think about that comment? If you were a customer in a hot market, would you decide to be loyal because you *like* an agent? How would you know you were supposed to be loyal? What's in it for you to be loyal?

(P. S. The other agent in our office and this agent discussed the situation. The second agent agreed not to work with the customer— even though the first agent really had no "claim" to the customer.)

Your Customers: Loyal or Not?

Your "position" about customer loyalty affects your self-esteem. Right now, what's your "position" on working with customers? Will you work with anyone? Do you expect loyalty? As an agent for eight years, I've tried it both ways—working with customers who work with other agents, and working with customers who are loyal. After having experienced the feelings that accrue from both arrangements, I decided to create a position of working only with those customers who would *agree* to be loyal. I found that, when a customer bought from someone else, I had bad feelings: Anger, depression, frustration. I didn't like what those feelings did to my self-esteem. What about you? What kind of feelings do you get from customers who buy from someone else? How you want to *feel* will determine what strategies you create about loyalty.

What's in it for the buyer to be loyal. Let's start with the most important human being here—the buyer. Can you list five reasons why it's in the buyer's best interest to be loyal to you? If you can't, it's awfully hard to ask for loyalty. After all, if *you're* not convinced, how can you sell the benefits to the customer?

If it was difficult for you to list five quickly, you're not alone. We did that exercise in a training meeting in our office, and it was pretty quiet in the room when we tossed out the challenge. As we started thinking, though, our group came up with these five:

1. You'll work harder when you know you have created a strong, long-term business relationship.

2. When you find a property that matches the needs of the two buyers, the loyal buyer and the "other type," you'll show the property to the loyal buyer.

3. Knowing you will receive long-term business from the buyer who is loyal, you won't be compelled to try to "quick-close" that buyer when they have seen fewer homes than they want to see—you'll patiently work according to that buyer's time frame, not yours.

4. You'll spend more time educating the buyer so that the buyer will be able to make an informed decision—not just an emotional one.

5. You'll work with the buyer as a consultant/counselor, not as a "quick-close" salesperson, because you are confident the buyer will buy from you when he or she is ready to buy.

After making your list and reading mine, compare the lists and use this information to create your explanation to the buyers about the benefits of loyalty. When we know why buyers should be loyal, we can put together a *process* for asking for loyalty.

When and how to ask for loyalty.   First, let's tackle *when* to ask. I like to explain to the customer during the qualifying interview that *both* of us are qualifying each other. The customer is deciding whether he or she wants to work with me, and I'm deciding whether I want to work with the customer. So, to get to know each other, we'll take a "trial run." I'll show the purchaser several homes. Then, at the end of that tour, we'll decide whether we want to work together.

When we get back to the office, I revisit that thought. I ask the customer how they thought the tour went. What were the services they appreciated? What would they like to see me provide? I get feedback from the customers so I know how comfortable the customers feel about me. Then, I summarize all the services I'll provide, and how they're different from the services of other agents. I attach benefits of my services to the customer. Last, I ask *directly* for loyalty. I've role-played this process on the audiotape, so you can hear how a conversation would sound.

The Biggest Mistake Agents Make with Buyers and How to Correct It

Are you using a questionnaire to find out what kind of home the buyers want? If so, you may be unwittingly leading yourself toward wrong conclusions! In most questionnaires, buyers are asked to give detailed descriptions of the kind of home they want to purchase: How many bedrooms, baths, etc. However, buyers don't make buying decisions based on finding the home that matches their descriptions. They make buying decisions based on *emotion.* That is, all those features that the buyers say they want in a home have to fill an *emotional need.* These emotional needs are called *dominant buying motives.* They include

- prestige,
- security, and
- personal space.

In your questioning, you must "translate" physical attributes of a home into emotional needs. For example, let us say buyers insist they need three bedrooms. So, you blithely search for three-bedroom homes. What they didn't tell you (because you didn't ask) is that they want a feeling of *privacy* by having two bedrooms on one side of the home, and the third bedroom on the other. Unfortunately, then, no three-bedroom home meets their needs. They're not looking for a three-bedroom home. They're looking for *privacy.*

Because most of our questionnaires ask only for features, agents don't learn how to keep asking questions to discover what these features are for. We don't question to find the *benefits* to these features. Finally, we have no way of determining what emotional need is going to motivate that buyer to buy. Bottom line: Unless we can light the fires of motivation, we can't "close."

From Features to Benefits to Dominant Buying Motives

Here's how to determine the dominant buying motive. First, using your questionnaire, ask the buyer about a desired feature. Then, attach a benefit. Then, surmise what the dominant buying motive may be. As you proceed through your questionnaire, you'll start getting a firm idea of what that particular buyer's dominant buying motive is. Here's the thought process:

Feature	Bridge	Benefit	Dominant Buying Motive
Large family room		Small	Family security
	So that	children will have	
		a secure place to play	

Look at the questionnaire you use. How many features does it ask for? Do you have a process to find out what benefit the buyers want from the feature? If not, when you find out the feature, ask, "what do you want that for?" or "what function will that fulfill?" or "what benefit will that provide you?" Write down the buyers' answers. Then, match the benefits to a particular dominant buying motive. For every buyer, there will be one most important dominant buying motive. If you want practice in attaching benefits to features and in sleuthing out dominant buying motives, *Up and Running in 30 Days* has a section and audiotape role plays for you.

Are Buyers Liars?

Buyers can be misleading. Actually, they don't know how to tell us what they want, so, when we ask, they do the best they can, but they can give us mixed signals. Roger and Margaret were from Ohio, and were being transferred to Seattle. They told me they wanted a newer home that would appreciate in value in a prestigious area. They wanted a view. They had two small children. Given the information I had, I took them up a steep hill to Horizon Heights, a prestigious area with views. We pulled up to the house, and I put the emergency brake on the car, because we were on a very steep hill. Roger yelled, "Margaret, don't let the children out!" Then, he turned to me and shouted, "Why are you taking us to *this* area? It isn't at all what we want. It's too hilly for the children. They can't ride their big wheels here." Well, by that time, I'd been in that car with the children long enough to imagine how fun it might be to let them rip down that huge hill in those big wheels . . . But, I was so shocked at Roger's reaction that I scarcely had time to imagine flying children. After talking a little with Roger, I found that, contrary to my assumption, *prestige* wasn't his dominant buying motive. His *family security* was number one. Roger and Margaret bought in a rural-suburban area with great schools, on a flat lot. Perfect match for *family security*.

The biggest mistake agents make is that, early on, they don't discover the dominant buying motive. Then, when they try to "light the fires of desire" to motivate the person to make a buying decision, they can't find the fire! Look back at three customers that you haven't sold. Do you know their dominant buying motive? Did you discover this early on and use it to try to "light the fires of desire?"

Make the dominant buying motive the *theme* throughout the buying process. In the initial questioning period, you must discover the buyers' dominant buying motive. Otherwise, you can't help them make a buying decision when you know they should be ready to make one. (Why? Because they don't have sufficient strength of emotion to commit to all that money for a home.) Remind the buyers of the theme throughout the buying process. When you're showing homes, bring that theme back by asking the buyer if that particular home fulfills their needs. The dialogue might sound like this: "Roger and Margaret, I know you told me you want a secure area for the children to play, because you told me family security is most important to you. The home we just looked at in Pine Acres is on a flat lot, with very little traffic. Does that give you the family security you're looking for?"

The best closing technique. By bringing back the theme as you show homes, review homes, and help the buyers to a buying decision, you are helping them check their emotions to assure that they do buy the home they really want. Remember, "sell the sizzle and not the steak." The sizzle is the benefit that satisfies the dominant buying motive. The steak is merely the physical feature. How the buyers *feel* about the home is everything. If you follow the feature-benefit-dominant buying motive theme, you will naturally help buyers make a buying decision. You won't have to worry about creating (and remembering) other "closing techniques." All you'll need to do to close is help them summarize their decision, remind them of their dominant buying motive, and find a place to fill in the blanks on the offer.

Analyzing Your Strengths and Weaknesses in Selling to Buyers

So you can get a whole view of how you proceed through the sales process with buyers, I've created Figure 7.4. It takes you through the sales process, which includes the following steps:

- *Attention*—What's your method of getting their attention (as in an open house)?
- *Interest*—How do you raise their level of interest in purchasing a home (by the questions you ask)?
- *Desire*—How do you provide an atmosphere where buyers can motivate themselves to make a purchasing decision?
- *Close*—How do you help a buyer decide on a home choice?

Ask yourself how skilled you are at each step of the process. Decide which areas need improvement.

Summary

In this chapter we've reviewed your approach to helping buyers. The first area we looked at was your qualifying process. Are you asking real qualifying questions? Are you being tough with yourself in working

Figure 7.4 Sales Process Evaluation

Using the information you've gathered about the selling process, review exactly how you take buyers through the sales or decision-making process. Write a self-analysis after each sales step.

Sales Process

Activity and Results

Step 1: Getting Their Attention

Prospecting for Buyers:
- How much?
- How?
- To whom?
- Materials?
- Results?

Analysis:_____

Step 2: Raising Their Interest

Qualifying/Interviewing Buyers

- How?
- When?
- How many per week?
- Materials?
- Loyalty?

Analysis:_____

Step 3: Creating Desire

Showing Homes/Reviewing

- How?
- When?
- How much per week?
- Creating motivation?
- Materials?

Analysis:_____

Step 4: Closing

Helping Buyers Decide to Buy

- How?
- When?
- Where?
- How much?
- Materials?

Analysis:_____

only with qualified buyers? It's the key to effective time management and to keeping your self-esteem. We also investigated how to differentiate yourself to quickly establish rapport with a potential buyer. Then, we helped you create a buyer presentation to gain further control of and respect from the buyer. Finally, we helped you capture loyalty for life. To end the chapter, we discussed the importance of attaching benefits to home features and sleuthing for the dominant buying motive. Following the recommendations of this chapter will put you back into the driver's seat with buyers, resulting in bigger commissions and more effective time management.

Your Tune-Up for Chapter 7

✓ Review your interview process with your buyer. Review your interview questionnaire. Add the "who, how, when, where, what" questions that are critical for qualifying buyers. Compare your questionnaire with Figure 7.1 using the considerations in this chapter.

✓ Using Figure 7.2, review the last three buyers you worked with. Write down your "posture" for working with buyers from now on. How qualified must they be before you'll work with them? Stick to your decision.

✓ Using the recommendations in this chapter, create three differentiations about yourself.

✓ If you don't have one, create a written buyer's presentation. Practice it with two colleagues.

✓ Write out your loyalty dialogue. Practice it with two colleagues. Get feedback.

✓ Review your dialogue during showings, after showings, and at closing. Are you bringing back the theme of the buyer's dominant buying motive? With your next three buyers, develop the dominant buying theme and "play the theme" throughout the buying process.

✓ Using Figure 7.4, analyze your whole selling process with buyers. Create an action plan for skill development.

CHAPTER

8

Top of the Line: Building the Value of YOU to Increase Your Confidence

Don't accept "old" beliefs. Think about what you do well; what you do that works; what you do that is a waste of time and resources. Concentrate on strengths. Build relationships. Be accountable.

Anne Bradley, CRS, GRI, sales associate

What are your strengths? What makes you good at the real estate business? If I were to see you and ask you those questions today, how many answers could you give me? How often do you think about your positive traits and skills? Or, do you mainly think about *why you're not capable*? In the real estate business, we have more opportunities to feel "down" than "up." When we're feeling down, we naturally concentrate on everything that we're doing wrong. To be sure we know *everything*, we take a negative inventory in our head—over and over.

To be successful in this business, though, we can't just think about our failings. Convincing sellers and buyers to work with us starts with our feeling that we're the best agent for that consumer. We don't get that feeling unless we constantly remind ourselves about our strengths. In this chapter, I'll show you a process to take inventory of *YOU*. I'll show

121

you how to use that inventory to promote yourself to buyers and sellers. Most importantly, I'll show you how to use that inventory to keep yourself up when things don't go right.

Standing Out from the Crowd

Not long ago, my husband and I attended a recital by the flutist James Galway. Because I have played the flute since fifth grade, I was excited to hear Mr. Galway. Since I took flute lessons from some of the finest performer/coaches in the United States, I looked forward to analyzing what made Mr. Galway so famous. Admittedly, Mr. Galway is certainly a talented, practiced virtuoso. But, so were my flute teachers.

What made Mr. Galway so memorable? His communication ability with his audiences. Many performers let the program notes do the talking for them. Not Mr. Galway. He took the opportunity to tell the audience, in a plain, down-to-earth, and humorous manner, the "inside" stories about the pieces he was to perform. He shared his love of transcriptions. (That means to take a piece of music written for another instrument, like the violin, and "musically translate it" for the mechanical constraints of the flute.) He told the audience how he delighted to discover, transcribe, and perform little-known pieces of music. He brought the audience into the musical world of the classics in an easy-to-understand way. It was then obvious how he had created his fame. What made him different was not only his musical virtuosity. Through his communication skills (including a charming Irish brogue), he could bridge the gap between the distant world of classical music and the "folk-art" audiences of today.

What Makes You So Special?

Mr. Galway has great technical and performance ability. Hundreds of flutists have the same level of performance skills. Yet, James Galway is much better known than any other flutist in the world today. His communication abilities distinguish him and make him memorable. It's my objective in this chapter to help you discover your talents in real estate, so that you'll be memorable. I'll show you a process to use so that you can really define the distinctive features and benefits of your service.

This differentiation isn't just for your clients. It's for you. The first person that we must convince we're special is *us*. To "change the rules" in casually addressing the audience, James Galway must believe that he has valuable messages to deliver—and that the audience will greatly enjoy hearing these messages. (If he doesn't believe it, he'll never have the nerve to try it!) It's the same with us. To be intrusive in a buyer's life (to ask him to be loyal to us), I must think I'm the best person for the job. Otherwise, how can I convince the buyer?

Confidence in *YOU* develops over time.   When I'm teaching new agents, it's apparent that they are unsure why anyone should list with them. After all, they're new in the business. Why should someone list with them, when they're not as experienced as another agent? Why should someone buy a home from them, when they haven't sold as many homes as an experienced agent? As you can see, this type of thinking is really a Catch-22. If I don't think I deserve the business, *when* will I give myself permission to deserve the business? There's always going to be someone who knows more, has more experience, or has sold and has listed more homes than I have. Does that mean that person is better able to help the buyer or seller? Not necessarily. But, the client or customer will never know why they should choose me if *I* don't know why they should choose me! That's not the end of it. Not only do I have to convince myself I'm the best person for the job. I have to create systems to show the client and customer that I'm the best person for the job.

When selling, remember to bring *YOU* along.   I have a friend who's a great speaker's coach. The topic of one of his presentations is, "When you get up to speak, take your body with you." From his decades of coaching speakers, he knows that, under stress, speakers forget to "be themselves" on the podium. They get all hung up on being "speakers," whatever they think that is. Unfortunately, many times the behavior that results is perceived by the audience as unnatural. Using low-key, effective coaching techniques, my friend helps speakers put *themselves* back in the picture—without losing the speakers' communication skills needed to impact an audience.

The same identity crisis happens when people become real estate agents. Since they've never been "salespersons," they can't imagine themselves in that role. So, they often try to be whatever "salesperson" means to them. This isn't necessarily a natural "fit." Then, the agents become uncomfortable, and search for a better "fit." Sometimes, they just reject any idea that's threatening their sense of self. That's why we hear salespeople say "it won't work for me in my area." What they're really saying is, "I can't see myself doing that."

Yet, to move into another field, we must learn new skills. If we close out all the new communication skills introduced to us, because they're "not like us," we actually never become an *effective sales communicator.* How do we move into a different life career, with new skills requirements, without losing "us?" The next few pages will help you do just that. If you're determined to put your career into high gear, if you've felt like a fish out of water, this information is for you.

It's not only what you will become that ensures success, it's what you've always been.   According to a recent survey of buyers and sellers, the three qualities they want in a real estate agent are (1) honesty, (2) enthusiasm, and (3) knowledge. So, relax. If you're a newer salesperson, you've hopefully already got two out of three—and you bring them with you from your *life!* It's just as possible to be lacking in sufficient honesty and enthusiasm—and the observer could see that in a person's whole life experience, not just how we act in real estate.

In other words, if we're dishonest in personal relationships, we're also going to be dishonest with buyers. (A truism: We behave in the future as we behaved in the past.) For example. James, an agent in our area, is dishonest in his business negotiations with buyers, sellers, and agents. His behavior hasn't changed. As a teenager, he stole from people's cars and homes. He uses his church affiliations shamelessly for business, while disparaging the "golden rule" in his business life. A reminder to all us managers: One's values "come with," both positively and negatively, as agents enter and practice the business. (True with managers, too.)

It's not exceptional knowledge that's expected.   Be wary of having a goal of obtaining lots of knowledge as *the* key to real estate success. Knowledge is needed to succeed in real estate. However, as we experienced salespeople have observed, the person who knows the most about real estate is not generally the most successful real estate salesperson. It's the difference between what's *expected* and what's *exceptional.* James Galway has great technical performance skills. So do other flutists. That's just an *expected* requirement for a concert flutist. Today, adequate real estate knowledge is an *expected* requirement of any real estate salesperson. That's not what makes a salesperson *exceptional.*

The old saying, "People don't care how much you know, until they know how much you care" is still true—and always will be. Being honest and enthusiastic is more important than having knowledge. After all, an agent could be knowledgeable, but dishonest, and harm the customer. In the past, have you acquired more knowledge about the law, regulations and rules, or "risk reduction," than you have acquired sales skills? If so, you've been trying to solve the problem of inadequate sales success with more *knowledge*. It's the other ingredient, "people skills," though, that separate the so-so salesperson from the very successful one. Be sure you're taking sales skills improvement workshops to hone your "people skills" to *exceptional*. (The Dale Carnegie Sales Course is excellent.)

People skills are the most important determinant of success. Most important to sales success (and life success) is a whole lot of emotional maturity, judgment, and just plain common sense. That kind of knowledge isn't gotten from a law text book or "knowledge-based" courses. This truism is borne out by studies in the book *Emotional Intelligence* (Daniel Goleman, Ph.D., Bantam Books, 1995). Goleman provides proof that high scores in intellectual intelligence (and knowledge) don't necessarily lead to business or life success. High scores, though, in emotional intelligence do. Such attributes as empathy, judgment, and common sense make up "emotional judgment."

Of course, our buyers and sellers rely greatly on us for "emotional judgment." I've known great agents to absolutely ensure a sale through their empathy, good emotional judgment, and common sense. I've watched these agents keep their cool under the pressure of a stressful negotiation. I've also seen very experienced agents stop sales that should have closed because the agents got emotionally out of control. For example, they stopped buyers from buying because they threw a temper tantrum at the other agent. They stopped sellers from closing on a transaction because they wanted to hurt the buyer's agent. I heard an agent one day "tell off a buyer" because the buyer had bought from someone else. The agent sounded like the petulant little boy who hadn't had his way on the playground.

None of this makes intellectual sense, does it? Agents don't get paid unless the sale closes. Agents don't do well over time without creating *good impressions*. It doesn't make logical sense to "tell someone off" because she or he didn't buy from that particular agent. But, as we in sales recognize, people make decisions based on their *emotional* needs, not their intellectual needs! To be successful, agents must have an abundance of emotional intelligence. Are you evidencing the traits of emotional intelligence as you work with stressed-out buyers, sellers, and agents? Are these instances where, if you had to do it over again, you'd interact with the parties differently? What does this say about your natural emotional intelligence? For keys to good—and bad— examples of emotional intelligence, read Goleman's book. It's fascinating and very revealing for us in sales.

Designing *YOU*

We've investigated the relative importance of the basic traits consumers expect from us. Now, let's start working through the process to design *YOU* based on your *life strengths*. Figure 8.1, Taking Inventory of *YOU*, shows the whole process: List your strengths, attach benefits to buyers and sellers of those strengths, and create proof that you possess these strengths. So that you can get the most from the process, though, let's walk through it, a step at a time.

Capture and Promote Former "Life" Skills

There are three areas of your strengths, exhibited throughout your whole life, that we're going to explore to *design you*: (1) Your life skills, (2) your life values, and (3) the knowledge you accumulated. The first area we'll work with is your business, professional, family, and "hobby" life skills. An example: I was a performance musician. One of the skills I developed as a result of all those years of performance is the ability to *improvise*. That means I can think on my feet—under stress. There were many times when the piano I was given to perform on had a pedal that didn't work, a key that stuck, or was so out of tune that Beethoven sounded like "saloon pieanner." Boy, did I learn to improvise! (I'll tell you why it's an important skill in real estate—later). Now, it's your turn. Using Figure 8.1, write down at least five skills you've seen yourself exhibit in your former business life, in your family life, and in any interests or hobbies. Remember, skills are *things you can do*. Don't worry now about why you're writing these or about what relevance they have to real estate. We'll get to that in a minute.

Analyze Your Life Values

Next, write down the values in each of those life areas that have driven your life. Think of what you love; what you avoid; of the "stands" you take. Get a list of at least five. You already know one of my values from reading this chapter: honesty. My example of James in this chapter showed my distaste for James's life values. Instead of manipulating people for personal gain, I like to help everyone win. That means telling the truth even when buyers and sellers don't want to hear it. Through their examples, my parents taught me that you couldn't live a *good life* and hurt people—in any area of your life.

Figure 8.1   Taking Inventory of *You*

Your Strengths	Benefits to Buyers/Sellers	Substantiations (visuals)
Skills		
Values		
Things you've done		

My dad had a meat packing plant in a small town. He told me that it's possible to cut corners in business and make money. He didn't believe in doing business that way, though. It's *not* possible to cut corners and be regarded as a good and honest person. It was most important to my parents to be regarded by their community, their family, and their business associates as fair, honest, and "good people." They were very *congruent;* that is, their behavior reflected their words. Personally, I find it hard to be deceptive, even when I would win more "political points" by being less straightforward. It's the only way I've found I can get through life without stressing myself out! Poor James. Although James tries to "cover up" his dishonesty and manipulation, it shines through in his behavior. Values, after all, are not what we say; they're the conclusions people make about what we do.

Recollect the Things You've Learned in Your Life

The last area we'll explore for discovering the strong *YOU* is in the knowledge you've acquired in your life. Write down blocks of knowledge you've acquired from your past occupation, your adventures, your schooling, your family, your accomplishments. Think of at least five areas of knowledge. For example, a woman who has raised five children has people knowledge and skills that are invaluable in real estate! By the way, you'll probably find threads of continuity and/or duplication throughout these three areas. Good. You're discovering your life themes. Your skills show what you do well; your values show what you think is important; and the things you've done show the knowledge you've acquired along the way. Next, we'll translate these "life experiences" to your real estate world.

What Your Life Learnings Mean to Customers and Clients

In themselves, you probably can't relate why some of the things you wrote are meaningful to your real estate career. Some of them may not seem to be applicable. No matter how farfetched, though, I suggest that you attempt to find some applicability. Why? I've found this common trait with successful agents: They're the ones who can easily and *generously*, at the *beginning* of their careers, relate and transfer their strengths to real estate success. They recognize that their life's abilities are going to help them be successful. They acknowledge that they are worthy of working with buyers and sellers based on their life's strengths.

Figure 8.2 The Cycle of Confidence

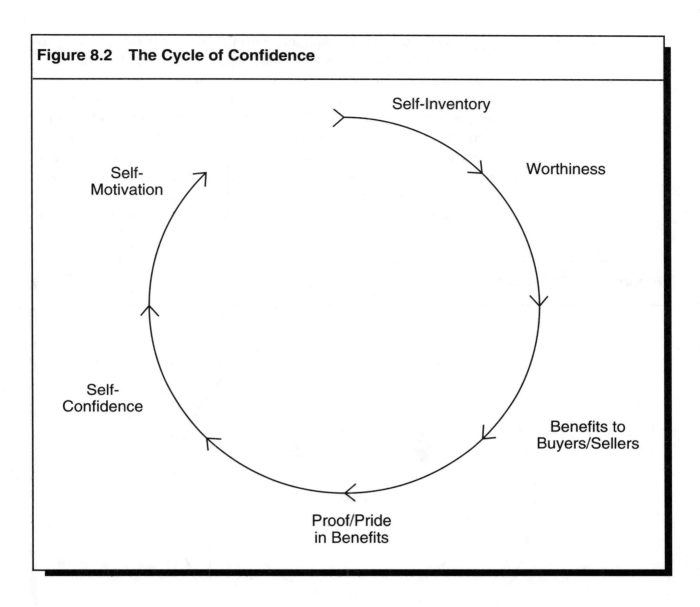

Then, this relating of strengths to worthiness creates self-confidence. Finally, this self-confidence shines through to convince buyers and sellers to work with them. (See Figure 8.2.)

Don't Forget the Benefits

We've just done the first part in this cycle: Taking inventory of your strengths. The next step is to translate, for yourself, why these strengths are valuable to your customers and clients. The "why it's valuable" is called the "benefit." For instance, a benefit of a fireplace (feature) is that it provides a cozy sense of warmth on a chilly evening.

When you state a feature, imagine each of your clients has a sign on his/her forehead that says, "So what?" (See Figure 8.3.) *Always* answer that "so what." Don't make your customer guess at what the benefit is. Brains don't work that way. I've found that the *biggest sales error* salespeople make is that they *forget to attach benefits*—in all sales situations. If we salespeople can't remember to do it, how do we expect the listener to attach a benefit? It's not natural. It's a learned skill. You, the salesperson, are the one who has to learn and practice the skill! This is especially important when you're building your credibility with a seller or buyer. From working with the strengths-to-benefits exercise,

Figure 8.3 So What?

"What's in it for the customer?"

Imagine that your customer is looking at you as you speak,
trying to figure out how what you're saying is beneficial to him or her.

you've seen how difficult it can be to relate your strengths to real estate. Yet it's of utmost important to acquire this skill and communicate the benefits of your strengths to potential customers and clients. After all, if you want to be known as *exceptional*, you must be able to communicate it. (You just can't walk up to a stranger and say, "Choose me. I'm exceptional. . . .")

Your Strengths to Benefits: An Example

Picture this. You're at the sellers' home. You're interviewing them to determine whether they're qualified to work with you. You ask what qualities they are looking for in a real estate agent. They say that they "want someone who will pay attention to the marketing of the property." They had a bad experience where the agent put up a sign and never appeared again. In response to the sellers, you say you know how they feel: "I was formerly the owner of four auto parts stores (Feature). Managing all those people and inventory, I learned the importance of a great marketing plan and clear communication. That means, Mr. and Mrs. George, that I have (Bridge) the experience and skill to create a much different, effective marketing and communication plan for your property (Benefit)." You've just followed the simple, yet most critical, sales communication process of all:

Feature → *Bridge* → *Benefit*

What **Not** *to Do*

Having given you an example of how to attach a benefit, I must give you an example of its opposite—naming features only. We adults sometimes learn better when we recognize the wrong way, and contrast it with the right way. I'm going to use this particular example because the majority of real estate agents do this the wrong way. This is what you most likely will hear as you listen to an agent answering a floor call:

Yes, that home has three bedrooms, two baths, and a garage. It has two stories, a large yard, and a fence. What else do you want to know about it? Okay. It has . . . , (and the features just keep falling out of the salesperson's mouth until he or she runs out of features). The caller says, "thanks," and hangs up. The salesperson attached no benefits, he gave away all the information, and he left it up to the listener to attach benefits—or negate features. Having received all the information, the listener has gotten what she wanted. She listened and negated the features she doesn't like or need (in her head). [Dear reader: The homes you and I live in have features we don't like. We'd refuse to make an appointment to see our own homes if the agent treated us like that!] Having not been engaged in a conversation, the caller takes the information and hangs up.

Selling the Benefits of YOU

Now, let's hear how a second feature-bridge-benefit process would sound, if you were promoting yourself to a potential client. Martha went into real estate in her forties, after raising a family. When meeting people whose family is important to them, she tells them that, not only is her family important to her, she learned skills that are beneficial to buyers and sellers. Here's her story: "I raised eight children (Feature). This means that (Bridge) I learned to manage many tasks at once. Being an effective listing agent requires that. Working with you, Mr. and Mrs. George, I can create and manage a marketing plan that attacks the market many ways at once. You'll get a faster, better sale with me at the helm (Benefit)."

Go back to your "feature lists," attach benefits for each one, and add dialogue.   No matter how farfetched they may seem, go ahead and attach benefits to clients and customers in each of the areas you've written. Now, start to notice the patterns. What stands out about you? What about these areas make you different from the average real estate agent? What skills, values, and life experiences should that customer and client value about you? Pick ten of these. Think of situations where you want to differentiate yourself from other agents. Now, practice the dialogue that would go along with this feature-bridge-benefit. Don't worry, you're not bragging. Bragging is making claims of greatness ("I'm number one") or throwing out statements like "I'm honest." Learning the process I've just explained is an "insurance plan" against bragging. When we attached benefits that are important to consumers, we're keeping their best interests in mind. By verbalizing this process, we're helping them find reasons to choose us.

We believe what we *see*, not what we *hear*.   Your last job in this process is to find a way to *show* the client your skill, value, or history. Don't be concerned about how you will package this information or deliver it now. Just think about how you could possibly *prove* you are what you say you are. Some agents are reticent to *show* buyers and sellers. Before you decide whether to *show*, let me share with you what

I have observed in a class as agents tried to differentiate themselves by *telling* or by *showing*.

In Advantage, my sales-producing workshop, I teach attendees to show proof of their claims. (I call this substantiating claims.) Some agents, though, prefer to try dazzle the listener verbally. So, I let the students judge the relative credibility of showing or telling. Then, they see and hear one agent explain his claims verbally. They see and hear the next agent explain his claims verbally and back them up with visuals. Invariably, the students (all agents themselves), choose the presenter who *shows* facts and figures, not just talks about them. Students judge the "showing presenters" as better prepared, more believable, and more trustworthy. Isn't that what you want your clients and customers to conclude about you?

How to Show the Benefits of YOU

Having worked through this process with hundreds of agents, I've found that showing it is where they get stumped. They're generally looking for some spectacular way to show the evidence. Not to worry. Clients are so thrilled with any backed-up information from sales-people that they're not sitting around critiquing the information itself. (It's only the agents that critique these systems—as though it mattered!) The clients are impressed because *you've got proof*—not what the proof is.

Here's what I mean. An agent in our office, Margaret, is very smart and very precise. She is a stickler for the details on purchase and sale agreements. Now, you and I know that some agents don't pay much attention to the paperwork. We would recognize Margaret as exceptional. But, when she meets a potential client, the client has no way of knowing Margaret's a real standout in this area. Yet, being a stickler for the details on purchase and sale agreements is a terrific benefit to clients.

So, how does Margaret promote one of her greatest strengths—and values to her potential client? One way would be for her to put evidence into her Professional Portfolio—her Book of Greatness, which demonstrates all the skills, values, and life experiences that differentiate her. She'd use a complex purchase and sale agreement that she created. She would write a short synopsis of this agreement, pointing out the special expertise it took to create and negotiate this agreement. Then, she could show a sloppy, horribly prepared agreement to contrast her approach with others. (Always protect the guilty—block out all names.) Last, she needs to write the *benefits* of this approach to clients and customers. Why doesn't Margaret just tell clients and customers she's good at writing agreements? Because clients and customers assume *every* agent is good at that. That's *expected.* But, we inside the business know that's not true. So, for Margaret to change the perception and elevate her value, she must create the feature-bridge-benefit of her skill and show exactly what that means to the client.

Be specific, offer contrast, and draw conclusions.   When you follow the feature-bridge-benefit-substantiation process, you'll be more effective if you offer specific examples. Why? Because we believe what *happened*, not what someone tells us *will happen.* Why have a contrasting visual? Because the client thinks that agents are pretty much all alike. That we all do business pretty much the same way. If you don't offer contrast (when possible), you'll be falling into the *expected* trap.

For example, a friend of mine listed his home with an agent in a small company. I didn't know Cliff was even thinking of selling his home. He obviously had not asked for my recommendations. (I think he thought we were all alike.) About a month into the listing period, he called me. He was furious. He'd gotten a copy of the brochure that the agent had created. It wasn't what Cliff would term a "brochure." It was handwritten, with misspellings, and looked as though it had been run off on one of those old mimeograph machines (remember the smell from school. . . .). Now, Cliff is an artist with wood. He builds gorgeous custom furniture. When you say brochure to him, his artist's mind goes to work, and, well, you can imagine what *he* thinks a brochure is. That isn't what he got. (Customers don't know what they're getting until they don't.) If you were competing with that agent for Cliff's listing, you would need to show what *you* mean by a brochure and what your competition's example is. You just can't do that contrast effectively without showing examples. It's *visual.* Since the majority of the population thinks in pictures, you'll want to "go visual" with your Portfolio and your marketing plan. Why leave it to chance that what's in your customer's mind is accurate? Another attribute of successful agents is that they work hard to *show* the potential customer and client what they will get. They don't just leave it to chance.

Other ways to show it.   Besides creating a Portfolio, these differentiations can be stated in a resume, brochure, and/or sales package. In addition to the written word, you can communicate your unique approach to the business through audiotapes, videotapes, and the Internet (and more ways coming up every day). You don't have to deliver all the information yourself. Your manager, other agents, former employers, affiliates (loan officers, title officers, etc.), and clients and customers can help you communicate. Think *creative.* Think *differentiation.*

When to Differentiate Yourself

You have all this material. You've arranged it in fine form, following the feature-bridge-benefit-substantiation process we've just explored. You've used alternative voices for delivery—besides yours. Now, you're ready to systematize the delivery of this promotional package. Remember how many times someone has to hear something before they remember it? About six times. You'll need to systematize your messages about six times to get real impact.

For buyers, you'll:

- put differentiation material in your prelist buyer packet,
- use differentiation dialogue when you first meet buyers,
- give buyers your Professional Portfolio on your first visit,
- use differentiation dialogue on your first visit,
- use differentiation materials in your Buyers' Presentation on your second visit,
- use differentiation dialogue during your Buyers' Presentation.

For sellers, you'll:

- put differentiation materials in your prelist package,
- use differentiation dialogue during your initial interview,
- put differentiation materials, including your Portfolio, in your first visit materials,
- use differentiation dialogue during your first visit,
- use differentiation materials in your Marketing Presentation in the second visit,
- use differentiation dialogue during your Marketing Presentation.

Recognize that the level of service expectations keeps escalating.   Once you've defined your strengths and attached benefits, you're well on your way to differentiating yourself. Don't rest on your laurels. Things never stay the same. Today, the client has high expectations of real estate agents. The client has many services that he regards as *expected*. In fact, the number of services that the client used to think were exceptional are now in the *expected* category (Figure 8.4). For example, few agents used to use visual marketing presentations. Now, many do. So, the client has come to regard the visual presentation not as *exceptional*, but as *expected*. Yet, as you know, there are many varieties of visual marketing presentations. Your challenge is to differentiate between an "expected" one and an "exceptional" one. To keep

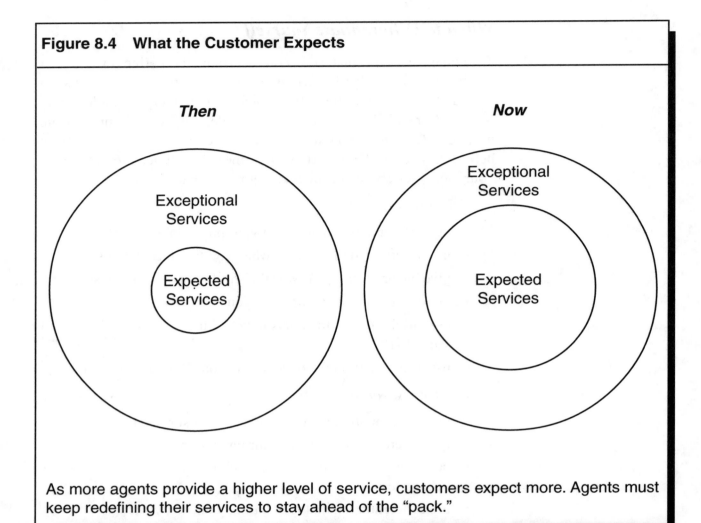

Figure 8.4 What the Customer Expects

Then

Now

Exceptional Services

Expected Services

Exceptional Services

Expected Services

As more agents provide a higher level of service, customers expect more. Agents must keep redefining their services to stay ahead of the "pack."

raising your standard of service, you must stay one step ahead of the competition. Here are some questions you can ask yourself as you create your visuals:

- Is this skill, value, or service exceptional?
- What do the clients think about it? Do they value it?
- Do the clients think it's expected?
- If I know my service is exceptional, how do I differentiate myself as providing a higher level of this service?
- How do I point out my level of service without reflecting badly on my fellow agents?
- What do I want my clients to say about me to referred customers and clients?

Listen to your own music for a quick confidence-builder. Now, you've packaged *YOU*. You've taken your skills, strengths, life history, and services and have imbued them with the sales communication skills of feature-bridge-benefit-substantiation. Get the greatest value from the hard work you've done. Read the information about *YOU* again each time before you get into the contact sport of sales with buyers and sellers. Remember, it's all really for *YOU*. When you're confident in your unique abilities, you're going to sell lots of homes to grateful, loyal people. Listen to your own music. It's unique. It's why you're selling real estate.

Summary

Creating *YOU* is a challenging, yet fun and rewarding part of selling real estate. When you start evaluating your strengths, it reminds you of why you went into the business. It's remotivating. I promise you, as you remember to put *YOU* in the business, you'll find meaning and value to the unique services you provide your clients and customers. After all, those services are unique because there's only one *YOU*.

Your Tune-Up for Chapter 8

✓ Complete the feature-bridge-benefit exercise about your strengths.

✓ Develop the dialogue that goes with the process.

✓ Develop the substantiations that differentiate you. Give them to your manager to help refine the ideas. Put them in a Portfolio.

✓ Package the substantiations so that you are communicating your differentiations at least six times with each buyer and seller.

9

Managers: How to Help Your Agent Get On Track to Success

Managers should help each agent analyze his strengths so that the agent can build on them. Provide the agent with the resources to incorporate into his business plans. Research programs that agents are successfully using elsewhere and help each of your agents implement them. For example, I encourage agents to attend the National Association of REALTORS® yearly convention; I help them plan their convention schedule.

**Laura Duggan, CRB, CRS, owner,
West Austin Properties**

This book is dedicated to helping serious agents increase their productivity and profitability. Although the program can be applied as a self-study, adding a coach to the program increases its effectiveness. The idea of "coaching" for business people is very popular today. "Training," long in vogue for businesses, has helped improve performance, but coaching—individual, customized help—is a much more powerful tool for *skills development*.

What is coaching? Coaches show students how a skill is performed. They demonstrate, they watch the student perform, and they evaluate the performance. It's all action. It's all skill development—doing it, not talking about it. The quickly changing business environment has put huge stresses on workers to gain new skills. The objective of coaching is a *change in behavior for greater performance*. So, there's a natural marriage today in the business world of coaching and skills development. A coach can observe our work and help us make changes for the better. A coach can help us sort through the myriad of information and make sense of it in systematized application. By applying the guidelines in this chapter, managers can use coaching techniques to help the agent gain greater success. The four-week plan in *On Track to Success in 30 Days* provides a proven system for performance enhancement.

My Survey Responses Indicate Need for Coaching

In preparing to write this book, I sent two surveys to respected associates. One was a survey for agents; one was for managers. On the survey for agents, I asked, "How do managers unwittingly hinder an agent's business?" and "What specifically could a manager do to assist an agent who wanted to take his or her business to the next higher level?" On the survey for managers, I asked, "What specifically do you do as a manager to assist an agent who wants to take his or her business to the next higher level?" and "What assistance would enable you, as a manager, to more effectively help agents gain higher productivity— fast?" Although the original outline for this book didn't include a chapter for managers, the answers to these questions were so insightful that I decided to add this chapter with the survey material, too. If you're an agent reading this, ask your manager to assist you in the manner developed here. If you're a manager, I hope you'll fully support your agent's quest for greater success through the suggestions in this chapter.

Must Managers Become Coaches?

Should a manager consider part of his job to coach an agent? To some of you, this seems like a ridiculous question. Why, of course, you say. It's a manager's job to help agents be productive and profitable. How do managers know they've done that? The manager creates profit on the bottom line of the profit and loss statement. But, does creating a profitable office mean that we're enabling each agent with us to be productive and profitable?

The methods in which offices create revenue do not encourage managing individual's career development. No. There's a difference between managing to create a profitable *office* and managing to create a profitable *agent*. The managers who actually see their jobs as creating careers *one at a time* are in the minority today. My observations are that, generally, the *actions* of managers indicate that they're as concerned about *each individual agent's productivity* as they are concerned about *office profitability*. Now, don't get mad and slam down this book, managers. I'm telling you my observations of *behavior*—not what managers *tell* me.

An example is the premise of the "desk fee" office. Desk fee offices don't depend *directly* for profits on an individual agent's *productivity*. In most desk fee offices, the agent has no minimum production required to keep a desk. As long as the agent pays his or her fee, the manager will retain the agent. (It seems hard to get fired for lack of productivity in a desk fee office.) The manager's objective is to fill the desks with agents who pay fees... the more desks, the more fees, the greater the profit. The fees the agents pay can come from anywhere—a spouse, a retirement plan, etc. The manager is usually paid a percentage of each desk fee. So, the manager is motivated to fill the desks. There's little in it for the manager to help the agents increase their productivity. In fact, some would argue that, if the manager does take time to help the agents build successful careers, the manager is taking away from his *recruiting* time.

In the short term, there's a positive result in a desk fee office with filled desks. It's profitable. In the long term, though, there can be other consequences. Many experienced agents today are not satisfied with their level of productivity. They're worried that too much of their hard-earned money flies out the window in expenses. They are caught in a quandary of low gross income opposite the need to spend marketing dollars, which they don't have, to increase their businesses (sounds like the small business person's normal dilemma). These agents need consulting help to spend dollars and effort wisely to increase their bottom lines. If the agent has no support for his career advancement, the agent loses motivation to get better. For most agents, there's both a *financial* and an *emotional* need to build production. To build a *career*, the agent needs to *sell*. (According to my surveys, even new agents expect to sell at least *12* homes their first year. Alarmingly, in my market area, agents sell, on average, only four homes a year!) Without sales success, agents become demoralized—and financially incapable or unwilling to invest in their career. They find other work, and their real estate career slides into part-time. Finally, they look for a cheaper desk fee office. They've now made real estate an avocation. It doesn't occur to them that they could have actually made a *career* of real estate with some management coaching and systems!

Now, don't think that I'm going to point out just the desk fee offices. My observations are that managers in more traditional fee structures today are using the same frame of reference for success, *office* profits. Their method of creating revenue is to hire *lots* of agents—the more agents, the better. So, their goal, like the fee offices, is to fill desks—the more desks filled, the better. After all, according to this philosophy, it takes lots of agents to generate a few sales. The agent isn't regarded as an individual with career promise. The agent is looked at as a "body" who will sell a few homes. Because many "bodies" are needed to make a profit, these managers are afraid to set minimum performance standards. With no minimum expectations, agents don't attain much. The result is *low per agent productivity.* It's simply Pygmalion: My Fair Lady in reverse. Pay no attention to them and they'll demotivate themselves. Still, there are some well-meaning managers who feel that they can coach each agent to higher productivity. The tides are turning toward this coaching management philosophy because too many real estate offices today aren't sustaining profits over a long enough period of time with the old philosophy of "Here's your desk, here's your phone. You're on your own." Managing each agent's successful career is the trend for it assures long-term profits.

The Result of Hands-Off Management

According to the National Association of REALTORS®, the average number of transactions per agent per year has steadily declined. What this means is *per agent productivity is declining.* However, because the agent captures more of the commission dollars, the *dollars* to the agent haven't declined. The alarming truth: Though agents have made as much money, they have created fewer happy clients. And, because an agent's long-term business is built on referrals, this "chasing dollars" is resulting in lower-producing long-term businesses. That's not the only result. We learn to sell by *selling.* Selling *motivates* us to sell more. To create an increasingly productive, delightful career, we must practice selling to motivate ourselves to higher performance. *We must stop chasing dollars and start chasing happy customers!* This means the manager must be involved in the process of creating higher sales production. We've tried it the other way. It hasn't been bringing us long-term profits.

The Successful Manager of the Future

The style of the successful manager for the twenty-first century will be similar in some ways and different in some ways from the past.

He won't be

- *autocratic* ("my way or the highway");
- *laissez-faire* (anything goes; just don't get me sued);
- *good old boy* (we're all friends here, okay? do whatever you want); or
- *hands-off* ("let me tell you, I don't have time nor skill to demonstrate to you").

He will be:

- *in charge* of setting the guidelines for minimum performance;
- *charged with choosing the right members* for a high-performance team;
- *a skilled coach*, demonstrating, observing, and giving feedback about the agent's performance to the agent;
- *a team leader*;
- a *facilitator* of ideas; and
- a *talent coordinator*, bringing out the strengths of each member of the team.

Julie Davis, CRB, one of the savviest real estate office owners today, says, "We must coach and counsel, not just tell them. We must lead by example. We must stay with them, coaching and counseling until the agent is capable of handling the situation by himself."

To succeed in the future, the manager must develop new skills: Coaching, counseling, demonstrating, facilitating. These are teaching skills. These are the skills needed for the twenty-first century that enable the agent to create higher performance. Looking at each agent as a *careerist* leads to the implementation of a long-term profit-making strategy: Ensuring each agent we hire is as successful as he or she *wants* to be, and as successful as he or she *needs* to be to bring us a per-agent profit. It's an insurance plan for long-term success.

Coaching the Skill of Selling

The key to a solid office is through creating solid, high-performing agents. Performance coaching is the only proven method for creating these successes. Although *On Track to Success in 30 Days* is designed to be used as a self-teaching tool for the experienced agent, it is much more effective when it serves as a system for a "coach." This idea of "coaching" is a new one to real estate. It goes against the grain of us independent real estate people. Many real estate licensees are self-proclaimed do-it-yourselfers. These are the kind of people who believe they can become first-class golfers without lessons. So, they blithely start to golf and quickly find out that their scores need improving. Soon, they get to the place where they can't improve their performance on their own. They hire a golf instructor, who proceeds to tear apart their pathetic technique and teach them all over again!

It's easy to assume there's nothing much to selling—after all, if you can *talk*, you can *sell*. New salespeople don't realize that selling is a *performance art*, a *skill*, just like playing golf is a learned skill. Most people who call themselves "salespeople," in my opinion, never really learn the *skill of selling*. They either underestimate the performance skills needed to sell, or think they can be "self-taught." There's one problem with coaching our own performance: We can't see ourselves as others see us. So much of performance excellence is created by the feedback we get about the performance—feedback from a competent coach.

I learned that as a little kid. I started playing piano by ear when I was four. For some reason, I crawled up onto the piano stool, picked out a melody my mother had sung to me, created the chords and rhythm—and played. However, I could only get to a certain performance level alone—by ear. Then I got my first piano teacher. With a piano coach, I greatly increased my performance skills. As I took piano lessons from more skilled coaches, my piano performance improved.

Just like playing piano, selling is a performance art. To get good at it requires a coach. The manager is the natural choice for a sales performance coach.

Coaching Ensures Performance Enhancement

Coaching to increase sales performance is a little-used instructional method in today's real estate world. I've discovered this by teaching would-be real estate instructors how to become coaches and trainers. Although most of them have some "teaching" experience, coaching *performance* is a new concept to them. As instructors, they've delivered information via lecture or discussion—they've *talked about* things—some ideas, some facts, some skills. But, talking about it ain't the same as doing it. Only *doing* it increases the skill. Talking about playing the piano does not bring the same performance result as playing the piano.

Talking about playing *is to investigate concepts.* **Playing** *is to increase skill.*

Because sales is a skill, the only sure way to get better at it is through coaching the performance of it. This is how coaching works. First, the teacher performs and the student observes. Then, the teacher observes the performer as he or she performs. Finally, both student and teacher exchange coaching feedback after the performance. This is the coaching sequence managers must use if they want to help their agents increase sales performance (Figure 9.1). Here's an example. Let's say your agent wants to develop skill in prospecting for expired listings. The coaching sequence is: First, coach demonstrates the sales call (he plays it) with the agent watching. Second, the agent demonstrates the sales call while the coach observes. Finally, both evaluate the skill demonstrated, make adjustments, and do it again. To "up" the pressure and performance, level two of performance would be for the coach to accompany the agent on a prospecting call for an expired listing. Going with an agent on a sales call is a much more effective method of assuring he or she attains greater skills than *talking* about going on a sales call.

(For a whole system on coaching, see *CrossCoaching*, my coaching handbook and audiotape series. It's a highly structured system for assuring that managers, coaches, and agents create coaching experiences that lead to peak performance.)

Coaching Is Part of Lifelong Learning

Through my years of piano and flute study, I've observed that the greatest performers never stop being coached. They're always looking

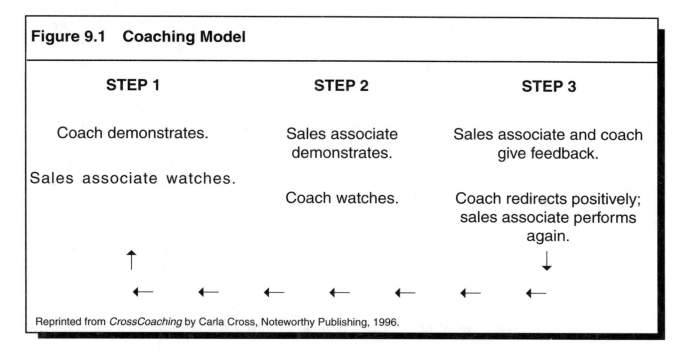

Figure 9.1 Coaching Model

STEP 1	STEP 2	STEP 3
Coach demonstrates.	Sales associate demonstrates.	Sales associate and coach give feedback.
Sales associate watches.	Coach watches.	Coach redirects positively; sales associate performs again.

Reprinted from *CrossCoaching* by Carla Cross, Noteworthy Publishing, 1996.

for another coach, someone who can help them perform to an ever-higher level. The very best performers are lifelong students. This keeps them fresh and humble. Oh, that we had that attitude in the real estate business! (Isn't it a critical attitude to have today in this era of revolution?) In fact, businesses internationally are finding that this concept of lifelong learning is critical for their survival and success. So, businesses today strive to create what they call a *learning environment*. That means that new thought processes and skills are constantly learned within the organization. Things are changing so quickly that all of us in any kind of business should be in a "learning mode"—dealing with change through implementation of new ideas.

Who to Coach

To create a successful office in the twenty-first century, the manager must pick careerists, use business systems, and coach to higher performance. Do all agents in our office want to increase their performance? We managers like to think so. So, we try to help them all, using great systems. But, some fail despite our efforts and despite the system. Here's the bald-faced truth: There are agents in our offices who don't want to learn, don't want to do better, and don't want to be coached to better performance—even when they say they do.

How do we find out who is "coachable?" The questionnaire in Figure 9.2 is to be used with the agent who is not meeting your minimum performance standards. It will help you determine whether you and the agent have the same success picture in mind. Here's how to pick "coachables." Sit down with the agent and ask him or her the questions in Figure 9.2. Probe for hidden agendas and objections to working the four-week plan to success in this book. At this point, you're *qualifying* him or her for your help, just as you want the agent to qualify potential buyers and sellers. Explain to the agent that you are using the same qualifying process that you expect the agent to use with his or her customers and clients. Ask the agent to review the four-week system you're going to use for regeneration. Tell him or her that, when you meet again in a day or two, you'll need an affirmation from the agent that he or she will work this system wholeheartedly.

Evaluating production potential. After your interview with the agent, use the questionnaire in Figure 9.3. Too many times, we managers dive right in, trying to motivate agents to change their sales behaviors. Now is the time to reflect on the odds for success with this agent. In evaluating the agent, be brutally frank with yourself. Don't set yourself up to beat your head against a stone wall with an unqualified

Figure 9.2   Evaluative Questionnaire to Agent

1. Tell me about a time in your life when you were down and overcame the odds. (You're looking for determination.)

2. In the past, when you really got into a project, what caused you to succeed and finish? (You're looking for tenacity and motivators.)

3. What, in the past, really got you down—to the point where you gave up and went to something different? (You're looking for motivators.)

4. Describe how you created a successful real estate business in the past. (Look for prospecting/sources of business.)

5. What are you doing differently now? (Look for habits.)

6. Describe how you are creating the business that you are doing now. (Look for prospecting patterns.)

7. How long can you sustain your standard of living at this rate? (Look for potential other sources of income.)

8. What would be different in your life if you had higher production? (Look for motivators.)

9. What would you do with the money? (Look for motivators.)

10. Where do you want to be in your life three years from now? One year from now? (Look for commitment to sales.)

11. What's stopping you now from re-creating the kind of business actions that created your prior success? (Look for priorities that would get in the way of prospecting.)

12. What are you willing to do to create _____ transactions per month? (Look for business creating activities in large numbers.)

13. For how long are you willing to do this? (Look for commitment of three months.)

Figure 9.3   Managers: Evaluate Your Chances of Success

Evaluation of:_____

(Agent)

Date: _____

1.   Has demonstrated ability to overcome failure.

2.   Is realistic about activities required, time frames involved.

3.   Has use for money.

4.   Will do the work required.

5.   Accepts personal responsibility for production.

6.   Can reach $ goal before savings are expended.

7.   Will demonstrate positive attitude to others while in program.

8.   Will be a long-term asset to office.

9.   Is worth the effort expended by the manager.

agent. Frequently, when managers start into the counseling process, the manager and the system are on track. It's only the agent that fails! If you're a good counselor, consultant, and coach, you must spend your precious talents on those who will appreciate and respond to those talents.

Let's go back to the qualifying process between you and the failing agent. After a day or two of contemplation, call the agent back into the office and explain your decision. Be willing to tell that agent that he or she isn't a good candidate for your coaching. Be ready to terminate that agent, if you've determined that your energies will not change his or her behavior.

How long to coach the agent who is not creating minimum production? Unless you're willing to coach that agent for at least three months, chances are you won't see any measurable differences in his or her sales results. However, to assure that the agent isn't deceiving you, be sure to monitor activities daily. That's what the four-week plan and activity grids allow you to do. Explain to the agent that he or she is on a three-month activity plan. Set minimum requirements for activities and results *in writing* with the agent. Make clear that you have the ability to terminate the contract *at any time*. Unfortunately, some agents take that three-month coaching period as a reprieve. They do no work for two months. When the manager questions those agents, they explain their understanding is that they have another month to get results. Stop that game before it starts!

Agents can use this evaluation process, too. If you're an experienced agent wondering whether to take the steps to revitalize your career, you can benefit from doing your own self-analysis. Use Figures 9.2 and 9.3. Doing this process for yourself will ensure that you stay in control of your own career path. Unfortunately, managers don't always involve their agents in this evaluation process. Instead, the manager decides that the agent is producing too little. He calls the agent into his office and tells the agent that he will be completing a prospecting plan. Yes, the manager's solution to the agent's low production is correct; however, the agent without partnering in the evaluation process now perceives the manager as an adversary—making the agent do activities he doesn't want to do. To ensure that the agent and the manager agree on the action to be taken and avoid an adversarial relationship, both must be involved in the evaluation process.

Evaluation tools. There are dozens of tools in this book for evaluating the agent's business. One way to use this book is to ask the agent to self-analyze his business and create a synopsis of his "business health" for your qualifying interview. In addition, there are two comprehensive evaluation tools that are especially valuable for managers' use. The first is the Listing Process Evaluation (Figure 9.4). This tool will enable you to find out exactly where the agent is strong and where weak. Then, you can diagnose and prescribe treatment. The second is the Sales Process Evaluation (Figure 9.5). This tool shows you how to diagnose an agent's sales process strengths and weaknesses, and how to prescribe treatment.

The simple reason most agents fail. If you've read the rest of this book, you'll know, from the quotes from my experts, their opinions are that most agents fail because *they fail to prospect* frequently and consistently:

- "They don't follow a well-defined prospecting plan for a full 12 months." Amy Dedoyard, associate broker
- "They're afraid to do cold calling and the prospecting needed to succeed." Jim McGuffin, sales associate
- "Lack of consistent prospecting." Lee Henderson, sales manager

Your biggest and most important job, as a coach, is to help agents create workable prospecting plans, help them implement the plan, help them monitor the plan, and praise them abundantly for working the plans. *Nothing is more important than prospecting to an agent's success.*

What managers need to watch out for in coaching. I asked my field of experts, "How do managers unwittingly hinder an agent's business?" Here are their observations:

- "They don't hold agents accountable to their goals."
- "Managers give agents bad advice to do lower productive activities. They should tell agents to concentrate on their past customers and people they know. Those are the highest-producing activities."
- "Some managers communicate expectations that are too low."
- "Hovering . . . too much control or too little . . . being uninformed."
- "Aside from hiring and retaining unproductive agents, their own 'bad' work habits can paint the wrong picture for those agents looking for guidance by example."
- "Some managers create or support an atmosphere that robs the agent of mental/emotional energy. The biggest favor a manager could do for his/her agents is to provide a supportive, positive environment."

Figure 9.4 How Professional Is Your Listing Process?

Below are the specific activities, systems, and processes that successful agents (20+ units listed and sold per year) perform to consistently list and sell 90% of their listed properties.

FIRST VISIT OR FIRST PART OF THE VISIT

	YES	NO
1. Prior to first visit, you ask five critical qualifying questions on the phone to determine that this is a bona fide listing appointment.	☐	☐
2. You go to only bona fide listing appointments.	☐	☐
3. You use a checklist to inspect their home with them and record the inspection.	☐	☐
4. You use a written list of the ten critical "seller qualifying" questions and note the answers in writing.	☐	☐
5. You give the sellers a packet of information that includes information about the company, the process, and YOU.	☐	☐
6. The information about you shows your specialties and includes testimonials. It addresses anticipated seller objections.	☐	☐

RESEARCH AND SECOND VISITS

	YES	NO
1. You use a method to design a specific marketing presentation for each of your sellers based on the information you got from the sellers on the first visit.	☐	☐

2. Your marketing presentation consists of two *equal* parts:
  (i)   The promotions you'll do (Marketing System)
  (ii) The pricing you suggest
	☐	☐

3. You use visual presentations for each of the two parts:
  (i)   A promotional portfolio
  (ii) A pricing portfolio
	☐
	☐
		☐
		☐

4. Your promotional portfolio shows at least ten special promotional tactics your company and office uses to get the seller's home sold.	☐	☐
5. Your promotional portfolio shows at least five *special* promotional tactics you personally will do to sell that home.	☐	☐
6. You have at least 15 pieces of evidence to anticipate and defuse sellers' 15 most common objections to listing with you at your price and commission.	☐	☐
7. At least half of your promotional portfolio consists of your specific marketing strategies.	☐	☐
8. You use a marketing calendar to show sellers when your marketing events will occur.	☐	☐
9. You give sellers their own special marketing plan—and ask them to approve it.	☐	☐
10. You use your promotional visuals to remind sellers that all those promotions work *only* when the pricing is right.	☐	☐
11. You have at least three visuals to show how listing at a lower commission assures the listing will sell at longer market time and lower price.	☐	☐
12. You have at least three visuals to show how taking your recommendations gets houses sold—at top price—and fast.	☐	☐
13. You have at least three visuals to show why listing at a higher price than your recommendations destroys your professional image while it hurts the marketability of the property.	☐	☐
14. You review pricing *after* you review your promotional strategies.	☐	☐
15. You use a written agreement of pricing, price reduction, and time frames that you have sellers sign when they list with you at a higher price than your recommendations.	☐	☐

Scoring: If you checked "yes" 18–21 times, congratulations. You're using the strategies that top agents have proven will work. If you checked "yes" 12–15 times, you're on your way to becoming a high performing listing agent who provides sellers what they want—a "sold" sign on their property. If you checked "yes" less than 12 times, use this checklist to sharpen your listing process, so more sellers, satisfied with your service, will happily recommend you to others.

Figure 9.5 Sales Process Evaluation

Using the information you've gathered about the selling process, review exactly how you take buyers through the sales or decision-making process. Write a self-analysis after each sales step.

Sales Process   **Activity and Results**

Step 1: Getting Their Attention   Prospecting for Buyers:
                                         How much?
                                         How?
                                         To whom?
                                         Materials?
                                         Results?

Analysis:_____

Step 2: Raising Their Interest   Qualifying/Interviewing Buyers

                                         How?
                                         When?
                                         How many per week?
                                         Materials?
                                         Loyalty?

Analysis:_____

Step 3: Creating Desire   Showing Homes/Reviewing

                                         How?
                                         When?
                                         How much per week?
                                         Creating motivation?
                                         Materials?

Analysis:_____

Step 4: Closing   Helping Buyers Decide to Buy

                                         How?
                                         When?
                                         Where?
                                         How much?
                                         Materials?

Analysis:_____

Here is some advice for managers on what to do to provide a career *boost* for agents:

- "Work out a twelve-month plan; check with the agent for ten minutes every week." Amy Dedoyard, associate broker
- "Help the agent with his business plan." Jim McGuffin, sales associate
- "Create and monitor an accountability system." Caroline Beason, owner
- "Managers must help the agent decide, 'Yes, I want to do this,' and must recognize that not every agent wants to change. You must help the agent stop old nonproductive habits and replace them with new activities and motivations." Heidi Medina, sales manager
- "Put the agent in touch with cooperative, helpful agents who have done it right running their business as a business." Anne Bradley, sales associate
- "Take the time to listen and explore where, why, and how an agent wants to go with their business. Be objective with constructive feedback, be 100 percent honest and 100 percent supportive. Help the agent stay on track and keep the agent accountable to their plan." Rick Franz, sales associate
- "Assist agent in designing a concrete, detailed activity plan. That broker must be in sync with his agents' aspirations." Karen McKnight, sales associate

Summary

Managers have heard agents in the last few years say they want to "go it alone." They don't need management. They're independent. Yet, their production has slid downhill, while their desperation for information and help has led them to course after course, expense after expense. The solution for higher productivity does not lie in more independence. Sales success, as in other sales fields, depends on

managers regarding each agent as a profit center, a business to be developed in each individual agent, and managers actively coaching and consulting each agent to help him or her realize his or her career dreams.

The quotes in this chapter have taught us that good agents desire and appreciate business consulting and coaching for greater success. It means to them that we care. To provide those services, we managers must develop consulting, coaching, and planning skills. The program in this book answers the need for a system on which to base those skills. Working with the twenty-first century philosophies expressed in this chapter, you can create a stunning, sparkling, vibrant office—an office that attracts the best and keeps the brightest.

Your Tune-Up for Chapter 9

✓ Use Figures 9.2 and 9.3 to analyze your career path, motivation, and long-term goals. If you're an agent, enlist your manager's advice during this process. Managers: Choose one agent in your office to complete the evaluation process. Get feedback from the agent regarding the process and your approach.

10

The Four-Week Plan to Propel You on Track to Success

Throughout this book, I've asked you to analyze your career from several perspectives. Now, let's put it all together in an easy-to-follow weekly activity plan that ensures your greater success. There are two parts to each weekly plan.

1. *Your business development activities (sales activities)*
2. *Your business support activities (organizing, skills development, etc.)*

You'll be using some of the analytical tools from the book in each of these categories to customize your plan to meet your needs.

Develop Your Business by Prospecting

We've heard the experts say, through quotes in this book, that the best way to increase your business is to increase your prospecting. So, using the *30 Days to More Dollars* prospecting plan (Figure 10.1), we will. This prospecting plan is proven. I use it for new agents. I've customized it for you with your experience level in mind. Your best sources of business are people you already sold or people you know.

Each week, you'll be contacting at least 50 of them to find out if they, or someone they know, need your services. In addition, you'll be getting "leads" from other sources of business, in the priorities and numbers easily laid out in *30 Days to More Dollars*.

In addition to your best source (old customers), you'll be getting business from certain other sources. These sources have been chosen because they provide leads to experienced agents in the largest quantities with the least amount of effort and expense. The prospecting priorities in *30 Days to More Dollars* are test-marketed and proven to regenerate the experienced agent's business. The second source, homeowners, uses a process called "circle prospecting." That means to contact, *in person*, each homeowner in an area where you've just listed or sold a property or you're going to hold an open house. The secret to success using this method is to visit each homeowner at least three times, until each feels comfortable giving you a lead.

The third source of business has been chosen because these are homeowners who have shown they have an immediate need for our services. Calling on them will increase your sales skills—and your bottom line. The last source is the only source where you "sit and wait"—open houses. To optimize your chances of a lead, do two things:

1. Increase your sales questioning skills.
2. Circle-prospect prior to the open house.

These four sources, worked in large numbers and combined with sales skills, will ensure your greater success.

If you need more information on how to make the prospecting calls recommended, I've audiotaped them and have written scripting in *Up & Running in 30 Days*. In addition, there are dozens of excellent sales audiotapes, books, and articles on prospecting methods and scripting. See your manager for suggestions.

Which Prospecting Plan Is the Magic Bullet?

New agents want to know *guarantees* of sales success. They want endorsement of a *certain method* of prospecting—before they'll start. They ask questions like, "Ms. Teacher, you just said that knocking on doors in a neighborhood is a good method to find buyers and sellers. If I knock on doors in the neighborhood, will you, Ms. Teacher, guarantee I'll make $50,000 a year?" It's not quite that simple (we experienced agents know that). First, you and I know that, if we do enough of it, *any* prospecting method will work! After all, it's first a numbers game. That's why it's so important to do the large numbers of prospecting calls in *30 Days to More Dollars*.

Figure 10.1 30 Days to More Dollars

Activity	Weekly Minimum

1. Contact Best Source First:
    Old Customers
    Former Professionals
    Affiliates (Mortgage, Title, etc.)
    People you know/meet
  In-person calls
  Phone calls
  (Send follow-up notes
	
	20
	30
	50)

2. Contact Homeowners with your Successes:
    "Circle prospect" *in person:*
    Go to homeowners in area to introduce new
      listing, listing sold, sale, open house
    Ask for "leads"
	25

3. Contact Immediate Sources of Business:
    FSBO: in-person or phone contacts
      or
    Expired listings: in-person phone contacts
  (continue follow-up each week with 20 calls)
	
	25
	
	25

4. Hold Public Open Houses (reactive) Adjust for area, time of year, etc.	1

Total weekly minimum in-person/phone contacts:

100 to 125

Second, we know that some methods work better than others for a certain neighborhood, time of year, etc. For instance, if lots of agents in our area are cold-calling and being abrupt with homeowners, our cold-calling efforts are diminished. (You used to think, when your phone rang at night: "Must be my best friend." Now, you think, "Must be a telephone company wanting me to switch.")

Third, we know that some of us are better at some methods than others. Some of us like face-to-face contact. Some of us like telephone contact. I'm not going to be a sales dictator and tell you *how* you must prospect. (I know agents love to prove someone else's prospecting plan *doesn't* work!) I'm not going to tell you the exact words to use. If you're talented and determined, you'll keep working at the skill of prospecting until you find out what works for you. Remember, sales skill is a lifelong practice. You'll keep finding new methods. The most important concept here to accept is that *practice makes perfect.*

Instead of worrying about which method is best and what exact script to use, just do it. After you do it, evaluate yourself. Take a coach along. Ask the coach to evaluate you. Keep practicing. Keep getting better. No great salesperson gets good by reading books about it. No great pianist gets good by listening to records. We practice, evaluate, add new technique, and do it again. That's how we all learn skills. If you don't accept this truism, you're looking for the magic sales bullet. Quit wasting your time. There isn't one. Yes, there is, in a different sense. It's *you*, experiencing sales!

Here is a prototype plan for sales success based on prospecting. I listed the variables to prospecting success. You can see why it's difficult to tell someone, "If you make 50 sales calls, in person, to people you know, you'll get 10 leads, 5 showings, and 2 sales. From my experience in sales, however, I know the best sources of business for you. I know consumer trends. I know what kinds of prospecting activities agents are willing to keep doing over time. I know what successful agents do. Armed with that information, I've given you a prototype plan for sales success by the numbers.

First, I translated the prospecting plan in *30 Days to More Dollars* to a grid, so you can see how this prospecting looks in a weekly plan (Figure 10.2). Then, I've continued the grids to include the results of prospecting. I've attached numbers to these sales activities, so you have an idea of typical "success ratios." Obviously, the reason to prospect isn't merely to get to know people. It's to get leads. And, the reason to get leads is to qualify those leads. Those qualified leads lead to sales and listings sold. The next grid, Monthly Activity Scorecard (Figure 10.3), shows you the numbers that should accrue from prospecting activities.

Figure 10.2 Joan Smith's 30 Days to More Dollars Plan

I've transferred the numbers from *30 Days to More Dollars* to the grid, to show you how an agent following the plan would set goals and log in results.

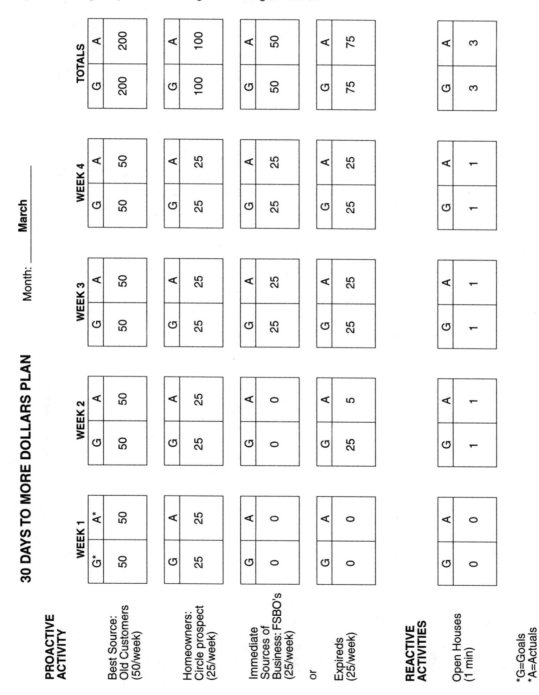

30 DAYS TO MORE DOLLARS PLAN

Month: _____ March

PROACTIVE ACTIVITY	WEEK 1		WEEK 2		WEEK 3		WEEK 4		TOTALS	
	G*	A*	G	A	G	A	G	A	G	A
Best Source: Old Customers (50/week)	50	50	50	50	50	50	50	50	200	200
Homeowners: Circle prospect (25/week)	25	25	25	25	25	25	25	25	100	100
Immediate Sources of Business: FSBO's (25/week)	0	0	0	0	25	25	25	25	50	50
or										
Expireds (25/week)	0	0	25	5	25	25	25	25	75	75
REACTIVE ACTIVITIES										
Open Houses (1 min)	0	0	1	1	1	1	1	1	3	3

*G=Goals
*A=Actuals

Figure 10.3   Monthly Activity Scorecard for Joan Smith

Here are the activity results for Joan Smith, who worked the *On Track to Success* plan.

MONTHLY ACTIVITY SCOREBOARD

Month: _____

	WEEK 1 G*	WEEK 1 A*	WEEK 2 G	WEEK 2 A	WEEK 3 G	WEEK 3 A	WEEK 4 G	WEEK 4 A	TOTALS G	TOTALS A
BUYER ACTIVITIES										
Counseling Appointments with Buyers	2	2	2	2	2	2	2	2	8	8
Qualified Buyer Showings	2	2	2	2	2	2	2	2	8	8
# Sales							1	1	1	1
LISTING ACTIVITIES										
Qualified Listing Appointments	1	1	1	1	1	1	1	1	4	4
Marketable Listings Secured	0	0	0	0	1	1	0	0	1	1
# of Listings Sold	0	0	0	0	0	0	0	0	0	0

*G=Goals
*A=Actuals

Before you start each week in this four-week plan, you'll be setting your weekly goals in each of the categories, from prospecting to sales.

The activity numbers and ratios that you create from your work are more important to your success than the prototype plan numbers.   When I was four years old, I sat down and started tickling the ivories. It didn't sound bad! Starting to play the piano was easy for me. I thought anybody could learn to play the piano like that, if they wanted to. Then, when I was in the fifth grade, I decided to add the flute to my performance repertoire (can you see me talking that way as a little kid). So, my parents rented a flute. For a week, I tried to get a sound on that flute. Finally, at the end of one week, I got a sound.

Was I discouraged that it took so long just to get a sound? No. I didn't know any better. I thought it took a week to get a sound on a flute, because all I had to judge by was my own experience. Also, I was very determined to play the flute. I didn't care how tired my arms or lips got. *I was going to play the flute.* (And I did, all through college.) Now, I know it doesn't take lots of people nearly that long to make a sound on the flute. I can show an adult how to make a sound on a flute in about two minutes.

The point is, we all learn skills differently. Some of us, like my son Chris, observe the skill first. Then, Chris practices slowly and perfectly, preferably without anyone seeing him. When we finally see him perform, it's picture-perfect. Not me. I just barrel ahead. Do it badly, and get better through trial and error. Other people frequently get better faster than I do. But, because I seldom give up, I end up being able to do that skill really well. How about you? What's your learning pattern?

Recognizing how you learn and how you get into action is important when you're changing the sales habits you've accumulated. The way to recognize your learning curve in sales is to keep track of your numbers. The grids explained above allow you to do just that. After you've spent a month setting short-term activity goals and results, you'll have enough statistical evidence to review your

- best sources of business,
- conversion ratios of prospecting calls to "leads,"
- conversion ratios of "leads" to qualified "leads,"
- conversion ratios of showings to sales,
- conversion ratios of listing presentations to listings, and
- conversion ratios of listings to sold listings.

Compare your sales success ratios to the prototype plan.   Armed with your sales success ratios, you can analyze how you're doing compared with the prototype plan I've provided. You can make adjustments in your numbers, target markets (the groups of people you're prospecting), sales scripts, and timing. If you want to attain greater numbers of results than the plan provides, simply "up" your numbers. The comforting part of knowing your own sales success ratios is that, when you need another sale, you know exactly what you must do to start the sales cycle (who, when, where, how much to prospect). Sales is not only a numbers game. It's an *individual's* game. I can give you a prototype plan and success ratios. You, though, must add your talents, learning style, tenacity, and analytical skills to create success your way. All great performers take what strengths they have and maximize them. They take their challenges and minimize them. It's hard work. You can do it. It's worth it for sales success.

Don't concentrate on the results—just do the activities.   It takes, according to the National Association of REALTORS®, about 13 weeks for buyers to find and buy a home. In our area, it takes about eight weeks, on average, for a listing to sell. So, let's say you find a buyer at the beginning of your four-week plan, and start working with that buyer in week one. If your buyer takes as long as the average, you won't sell that buyer a home within four weeks. Don't be disappointed. This is a long-term business for results.

But, to make sure we're on the right track to results, we must focus and keep track of the sales-producing activities. If we're doing few activities, it would be just "dumb luck" that we'd sell something to someone. My observations are that some agents rely on "dumb luck" to make money in real estate. They must think it's an easy business, where people just show up with checkbooks. You and I know that's not true! Keeping track of your activities and doing self-analysis of them will teach you the invaluable self-management skills that great performers all have developed.

How to Get the Prospecting Plan Started

In Chapter 4, you did an analysis of your sources of business. I'm including it again here (Figure 10. 4) so that you can compare it to the sources in the prototype prospecting plan, *30 Days to More Dollars Plan*. With those figures side by side, make any adjustments needed to the prototype plan to reflect your best sources of business. For instance, if you got lots of business from making calls on your former business associates, include that in the customization of your *30 Days to More Dollars Plan*. Make sure you include only *proactive* prospecting activities. For example, say you completed nine total transactions last

Figure 10.4 A Review of Your Business

Sales _____ Listings taken (LT) _____

Listings sold (LS) _____ % of LT to LS _____
_____

Average time on market for your listings: _____ (Breakdown by price range if desired)

% of sales price to list price for your listings _____   Number of new listings sold _____

Number of resales sold _____   Number of resale listings sold _____

Number of new homes sold _____

Origination of Buyers/Sellers		
	Buyers	Sellers
Reactive prospecting		
Floor time		
Open houses		
Proactive Prospecting (Segmented by Target Market)		
Old Customers/Clients		
First-Time buyers		
Move-up buyers		
Transferees		
Empty-Nesters		
Geographical farm		
Prior business contacts		
Builders		
Other:_____		

Of these sellers, which market gave you the most sold listings?

☞ **Keep exploiting these markets. They're your most effective.**

year. Six of those transactions came from floor time (reactive). Some agents might think, "Well, then, I'll increase my floor time." This is a common mistake agents make. They rely on people calling *them* to create business. But, what if no one calls? The market may have changed; the consumer may have changed; maybe you or your office can't afford to place as many ads in the newspaper as before. Instead of trying to increase the amount of time you sit and wait for a customer, go out and find customers. Then, you're always in control of your destiny. Remember, it's a *numbers* game, not a *time* game. To prepare your weekly plan, take the numbers and sources of business you customized on *30 Days to More Dollars*, and put them in the blank sales activity grids (Figures 10.10 and 10.11) at the end of the four-week plan. These numbers are your personalized goals for each week.

Do you have to do the number of sales calls recommended in each category in *30 Days to More Dollars* to get enough leads? Your best source of leads, by far, is the first category: Old customers and clients, with subcategories of former professionals, affiliates (mortgage, title cos., etc.) and people you know and meet. Why? Because we all like to do business with people we know and trust. If you can find enough people in this category to support the rest of the sales activities numbers you want, you needn't use any other prospecting methods.

Here's what I mean. Let's say you have 200 old customers and clients, whom you haven't been calling for leads. You start calling them, setting a goal of 50 per week. They deliver to you five qualified buyers and five qualified sellers in week one. That's probably enough for you to work with and get at least one sale and one listing by the end of the four weeks. Then, in week two, you contact another 50 more. You get the same number of qualified buyers and sellers. You're proving to yourself that, for you, your best source for leads to deliver your desired results is all in category one. But, wait a minute. Suppose you want to expand your results—get more sales and listings sold. But, you've already exhausted your potential supply of leads in category one. Then, move to the other categories. Agents make two mistakes in prospecting:

1. They don't optimize their best source of leads (category one).
2. They don't expand their target markets to other sources of leads when they need to in order to get the increased results they desire.

So, keep track of your numbers, and from whence they come. Be ready to prospect in as many markets as you need to be in order to assure the number of sales and listings sold you expect. When in doubt, use my categories, priorities, and numbers. They work.

Establish Your Weekly Prospecting Schedule

By using the figures in Chapter 1, you've done the analysis on the state of your business. You've done a comparison between the successful agent's weekly schedule and yours. You've established numbers for the sales activities for each week. Your next step is to establish a weekly schedule. Many of the things that go into your schedule are listed in each week of the weekly plan. To help you get the habits of prioritization for sales success, I've separated "business development" activities from "business support" activities. Before you start each week, put each of the assignments from the weekly plan in your weekly schedule. I've provided a grid for each week (Figure 10.5). Writing your weekly schedule before you start your week is an extremely important step toward greater success. In consulting with hundreds of agents who want to increase their business, one thing they have in common is that they don't create a weekly schedule—prior to the week starting. With no schedule, they come to work on Monday and wait for someone to schedule them! Of course, because only four to ten hours a week is scheduled by the office for each agent, those agents have lots of time on their hands! To get into the habit of scheduling *you*, make out your schedule and pretend that some tough, hard-nosed boss is handing the schedule to you each day, threatening to fire you if you don't complete the schedule. That tough, hard-nosed boss is *you*!

Congratulate Yourself Each Week for Your Success

There are three things you'll want to accomplish each week in this four-week plan:

1. Set your weekly goals; keep track of the results.
2. Create a weekly schedule and follow it.
3. Complete all the business development and business support activities.

Having accomplished each of these activities, reward yourself. Set up some system of congratulation and appreciation for yourself, just like an "outside" boss would congratulate you. Remember, you've got a tough, hard-nosed boss—but a fair one. Fair bosses recognize and reward desired behavior. Because you're the boss and the employee, you get to reward yourself in whatever way is meaningful to you. Be sure to do this each week, so you're motivated to keep doing the plan to greater success. Tell your manager your successes, so he or she can share in them with you. We managers are thrilled when agents take themselves by the collar of the jacket, shake themselves up, and create success. After all, we can't *make* anyone do this plan. However, we can assist, support, and congratulate someone who's changing his or her sales habits for the better.

Figure 10.5   Your Weekly Plan

Your Weekly Plan

Name: _____

Week: _____

Time	Monday	Tuesday	Wednesday	Thursday	Friday	Saturday	Sunday
7-8							
8-9							
9-10							
10-11							
11-12							
12-1							
1-2							
2-3							
3-4							
4-5							
5-6							
6-7							
7-8							
8-9							

Week One: Success Plan

Daily Plan

Make your daily plan for the week. I've created a grid for you here (Figure 10.6). Follow these guidelines:

- First, put in office-scheduled events (office meeting, tour). You're on the team first.
- Second, log in business-producing activities (qualifying buyers and sellers, showings, listing presentations, sales, listings, listings sold as goals from each of these week's assignments).
- Third, log in prospecting activities (from *30 Days to More Dollars Plan*).
- Fourth, log in floor time and open house (don't overdo these).
- Fifth, log in meeting with manager to share successes.
- Sixth, log in business support activities.

Make your daily schedule for the week the same way for each of these four weeks, until you develop this *success habit*.

Business Development: Week One

Do the *30 Days to More Dollars* prospecting plan. Set goals on the activity grid at the back of this section (Figure 10.10). Keep track of your successes. Analyze your success ratios.

Using the second grid at the back of this section, Monthly Activity Scoreboard (Figure 10.11), set these goals for results from your prospecting plan:

- Find two qualified buyer "leads."
- Locate two qualified seller "leads."
- Put customers in your car at least twice.
- Schedule and give one listing presentation.

Figure 10.6   Your Weekly Plan: Week One

Your Weekly Plan

Name: _____

Week: _____

Time	Monday	Tuesday	Wednesday	Thursday	Friday	Saturday	Sunday
7-8							
8-9							
9-10							
10-11							
11-12							
12-1							
1-2							
2-3							
3-4							
4-5							
5-6							
6-7							
7-8							
8-9							

Business Support: Week One

Increase your sales skills.   Read two sales books. Listen to sales audiotapes 20 minutes per day, five days per week. Apply two new sales skills this week when you work with buyers and sellers.

Increase your skills with buyers.   Complete a visual Buyers' Presentation. Practice it. Practice asking for loyalty. Analyze your success ratios with buyers. Do you need to qualify better? If so, put better qualifying methods into your Buyers' Presentation. Review the details of working with buyers in the earlier chapters. Incorporate two ideas from these chapters into your "buyer repertoire."

Increase your skills with sellers.   Review your whole listing process, using Figure 6.3. Begin your plan to tighten your process for more effectiveness. Prepare a prelist packet for sellers.

Be sure the sellers' packet has at least five messages that anticipate objections you think you may get later. Be sure to include at least three differentiations about you.

Keeping your spirits up: Read one motivation book. Write one motivational thought in your motivational notebook each day of this week. Give yourself positive self-talk each day.

Week Two: Success Plan

Make your daily plan for the week, using the guidelines in week one. Use the grid provided here (Figure 10.7). At the end of the week, grade yourself on how well you followed your plan. Decide what to watch for in week three.

Business Development: Week Two

Continue the *30 Days to More Dollars* prospecting plan. Customize it for your needs and successes. Set your goals on the grids in the back of this section (Figures 10.10 and 10.11). Write your results. Analyze the outcomes and make changes for your needs.

Using Figure 10.11 in the back of this section, set these goals for sales results:

- Two qualified buyer appointments
- Two showing appointments with buyers
- Two qualified seller "leads"
- One qualified listing presentation

Keep track of your results. Are you hitting your mark? What numbers do you need to adjust? Do so for week three.

Business Support: Week Two

Increase your sales skills. Read one sales book this week. Listen to two audiotapes. Incorporate two sales skills in your working with buyers and sellers. Teach a new agent one of the sales skills you're using now (the best way to learn is to teach!).

Increase your skills with buyers. Put together a premeeting buyer information packet. Practice dialogue to introduce this packet to potential buyers. Differentiate yourself while you introduce this packet. Be sure the themes of the packet are carried through in your Buyer Presentation package. Are you discovering the dominant buying motive in your buyer counseling session? This week, while you work with buyers, bring back their "dominant buying motives" as you show each home. You're preparing to help them "light the fires of desire" as they find the home of their dreams (so you can close them).

Increase your skills with sellers. Put together a marketing presentation. Include at least ten visuals that anticipate sellers' most common objections. Practice your sales dialogue for this presentation. Review the last three listings you didn't get. Analyze the objections you couldn't anticipate or answer. Using this information, create your marketing presentation.

Keep your spirits up. Read another motivational book this week. Listen to a motivational tape. Talk to someone who's always "up." Write one motivational message to yourself each day in your notebook. Give yourself at least five positive self-messages each day this week.

Figure 10.7   Your Weekly Plan: Week Two

Your Weekly Plan

Week: _____   Name: _____

Time	Monday	Tuesday	Wednesday	Thursday	Friday	Saturday	Sunday
7-8							
8-9							
9-10							
10-11							
11-12							
12-1							
1-2							
2-3							
3-4							
4-5							
5-6							
6-7							
7-8							
8-9							

Week Three: Success Plan

Make your daily plan for the week, using the guidelines in week one. Use the grid provided here (Figure 10.8). At the end of the week, grade yourself on how well you followed your plan. Decide what to watch for in week four.

Business Development: Week Three

Add one new source to your potential prospects: Other agents. First, make a list of 50 agents you think would refer to you. Call all 50 of them and ask for referrals. Keep track of the results. This is another customization of your *30 Days to More Dollars Plan*.

Continue the *30 Days to More Dollars* prospecting plan. Customize it for your needs and successes. Set your goals on the grids in the back of this section (Figures 10.10 and 10.11). Write your results. Analyze the outcomes and make changes for your desired results.

Using the second grid in the back of this section, set these goals for sales results:

- Get two qualified buyer appointments.
- Show homes to two qualified buyer groups.
- Get two appointments to do a listing presentation.
- List one marketable property.

Keep track of your results. Are you hitting your mark? What numbers do you need to adjust? Do so for week four.

Business Support: Week Three

Increase your skills with buyers. Create a Professional Portfolio to use with buyers and sellers. Follow the procedure in Chapter 8 for assembling a Portfolio that reflects your strengths, values, and skills. Use the Portfolio with buyers and sellers in week three and week four.

Increase your skills with sellers. Create visuals and dialogue for the pricing part of your presentation. Start with market trends and work to the specific homes in the area. Reflect back to your prelist materials and

Figure 10.8   Your Weekly Plan: Week Three

Your Weekly Plan

Name: _____

Week: _____

Time	Monday	Tuesday	Wednesday	Thursday	Friday	Saturday	Sunday
7-8							
8-9							
9-10							
10-11							
11-12							
12-1							
1-2							
2-3							
3-4							
4-5							
5-6							
6-7							
7-8							
8-9							

marketing presentation to make sure that you have enough information to anticipate pricing objections. Practice the dialogue.

Keep your spirits up.   Continue reading your motivational books. Subscribe to one sales/motivational magazine and read it this week. Write in your notebook. Give yourself positive self-talk. Ask your manager for three "positive strokes," compliments. You deserve them! The best agents I know are able to ask for a compliment with grace and confidence. After all, if we want appreciation, what's a better way to make sure we get it?

Week Four: Success Plan

Make your daily plan for the week, using the guidelines in week one. Use the grid provided here (Figure 10.9). At the end of the week, grade yourself on how well you followed your plan. Decide what to watch for as you continue your work for greater success.

Business Development: Week Four

Continue doing the prospecting plan in *30 Days to More Dollars*. By now, you should be finding out that you have an overabundance of "leads." So, you have an enviable problem: To assure you don't run yourself ragged, you must be tougher in qualifying buyers and sellers. Throughout this program, I've provided you with methods of being kind but tough. This week, concentrate on qualifying. This week, draw conclusions from your numbers in this four-week success plan. What are your best sources of leads? How can you optimize them throughout the rest of your career?

Using the grids in the end of this chapter (Figures 10.10 and 10.11), set your activity goals for this week. These should be, at least:

- Get two listing appointments with qualified sellers.
- Get two showing appointments with qualified buyers.
- Sell one home.

Keep track of your activities this week. Analyze your results. What adjustments do you need to make to your prospecting plan to assure you get the results you want?

Figure 10.9   Your Weekly Plan: Week Four

Your Weekly Plan

Name: _____

Week: _____

Time	Monday	Tuesday	Wednesday	Thursday	Friday	Saturday	Sunday
7-8							
8-9							
9-10							
10-11							
11-12							
12-1							
1-2							
2-3							
3-4							
4-5							
5-6							
6-7							
7-8							
8-9							

Figure 10.10   Your 30 Days to More Dollars Plan

30 DAYS TO MORE DOLLARS PLAN

Month: _____

PROACTIVE ACTIVITY	WEEK 1		WEEK 2		WEEK 3		WEEK 4		TOTALS	
	G*	A*	G	A	G	A	G	A	G	A
Best Source: Old Customers (50/week)										
Homeowners: Circle prospect (25/week)										
Immediate Sources of Business: FSBO's (25/week)										
or										
Expireds (25/week)										
REACTIVE ACTIVITIES										
Open Houses (1 min)										

*G=Goals
*A=Actuals

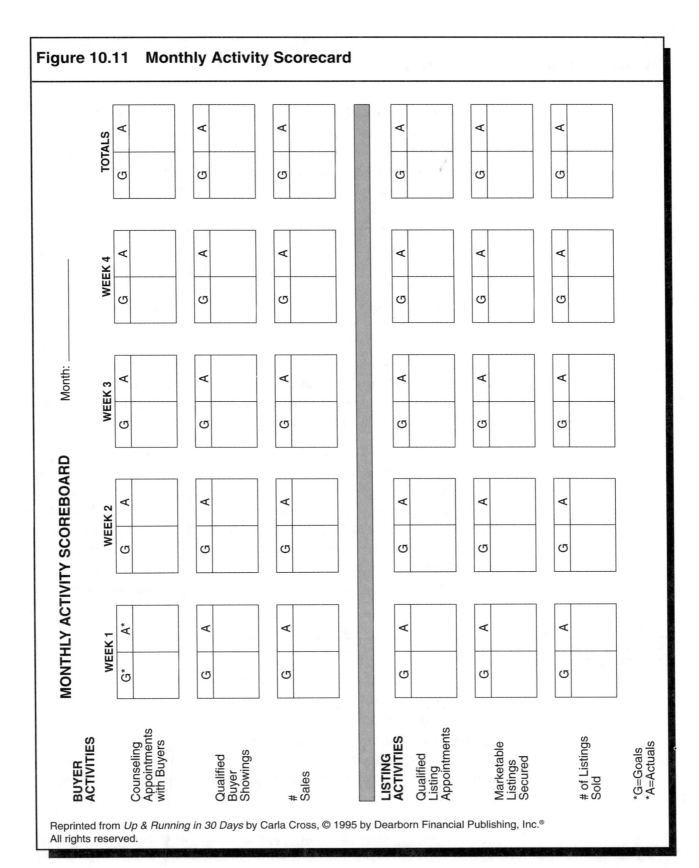

Figure 10.11   Monthly Activity Scorecard

Business Support: Week Four

Increase your skills with buyers.   You've created a process to educate buyers (prelist package). You've create a process with visuals to educate and qualify buyers (buyer presentation*).* You've created differentiators about yourself through your Professional Portfolio. You've developed interview techniques to attach benefits and discover dominant buying motives. How's your ability to help buyers make a decision? Are you lighting the fires of desire and helping buyers make a choice? If your skills here are not as good as you'd like, review the chapters in the sales books you've been reading on "closing."

A note: In this day and age, closing techniques aren't nearly as important as the questioning techniques employed in the getting-to-know-you phase of the buyer sales cycle. Review your method of working with buyers from start to end, using the analytical tool, Sales Process Evaluation, in Chapter 7. Where are your strengths? Your weaknesses? Set up a long-term program to become a skilled salesperson working with buyers. In the future, with Buyer Agency, you can't afford not to be as skilled with buyers as you are with sellers.

Increase your skills with sellers.   By now, you should have more seller appointments for listings than you can handle. How are you qualifying these appointments? Are you tough enough? Do you want to be known as a listing agent or as an agent who gets listings sold? Only the latter will allow you to build a promotable success record. Build a long-term plan now, based on your professional guidelines for listing properties. Hit the highest mark for yourself in professionalism. List only marketable properties. You'll create a more delightful, rewarding career.

Summary

Congratulations! You've really retooled your career. You've had the intestinal fortitude (well, okay, guts) to look at your work habits realistically. You've been brave enough to compare these work habits to those of more successful agents. You've made the necessary adjustments in your short-term business plan. You've created the support materials and dialogue that very successful agents use to project confidence and professionalism. Throughout the process, you've kept yourself "up" by congratulating yourself and adding outside sources of inspiration. You're on your way to a much more rewarding career—rewarding not only in a monetary way, but in a life-inspiring way: With your new dedication to excellence, you're creating long-term professional relationships that help develop all lives affected by your approach (yours, too).

To close, let me bring back my panel of experts. They have some overall advice and encouragement for you:

- "Put your plan in writing—NOW—and commit to doing it. You have to be proactive. Be out there meeting new prospects and follow a system for contacting them consistently." Karen McKnight, sales associate

- "Treat your business like the professional career it is. Develop good work habits that you can sustain over the long haul. This requires superior time-management/self-management skills that are appropriately balanced with family, social, and personal time." Julie Davis, owner

- "Know what it is you want and how you plan to get it. Believe and buy into your goals, review them daily, and persist in never giving up till you've gotten where you want to go. Surround yourself with people who are only positive influences along the way." Rick Franz, sales associate

- "Yesterday is over. Give yourself 20 minutes to rail and scream and whine about lost opportunities, rejection, disappointments; then, put it behind you and move on. Do proactive, result-oriented activities. Act cheerful. Smile. Don't keep doing activities that don't work. Connect with someone to whom you can be accountable. Plan your time and do the activities you plan." Anne Bradley, sales associate

And, finally, an especially inspiring thought from my friend, Heidi Medina, sales manager, who wrote *four single-spaced pages* in answering my survey. She really cares about your success, and about our profession. Here's Heidi:

- "Have fun and laugh every day. Decide to like your work and focus on what it does for you, not to you. Dream a lot! Write down your perfect day in great detail, events that would happen in your perfect life. Learn to write good affirmations and then use them. Each and every morning review your affirmations. Remember that it's your life. You have to take control of the wheel or you will just keep on spinning."

Take control of the wheel. Get on track to greater success. I know this program will help you do just that. You're on your way to creating an ever more successful career—and life. As you capture your version of success, let me know. I love to hear how others have used my programs to get where they want to go. I want you to be so successful that I'll be quoting you, like the people I've quoted above, in my next book! It will be your turn, and privilege, to inspire others to effect their own success.

References

Reaching Your Career Objectives

CrossCoaching. Carla Cross. Noteworthy Publishing, 1996. A 150-page handbook that explains exactly how to coach, how to manage programs, new agents' role. All checklists included. Three audiotapes explain program from each participant's view. A coaching companion to *Up & Running in 30 Days* and *On Track to Success in 30 Days*.

How about a Career in Real Estate? 2nd edition. Carla Cross. Noteworthy Publishing, 1996. Endorsed and recommended by the Real Estate Brokerage Managers Council.

List the Buyer System. Issaquah, Wash.: Carla Cross Seminars, 1995. Includes a 24-page buyer's presentation to raise your value, plus insider tips on how to control buyers and get loyalty for life.

The Real Estate Agent's Business Planning Guide. Carla Cross. Chicago: Real Estate Education Company, Inc.®, 1994. Endorsed and recommended by the Real Estate Brokerage Managers Council.

The Real Estate Business Planning System. Issaquah, Washington: Carla Cross Seminars, 1996. Three series of audiotapes provide personal business plan consulting: Series 1, For Agents Without a Plan; Series 2, For Agents With a Plan; Series 3, For Managers. Four tapes in each series. Endorsed and recommended by the Real Estate Brokerage Managers Council. 800-296-2599.

Up & Running in 30 Days. Carla Cross. Chicago: Real Estate Education Company, Inc.®, 1995. Endorsed and recommended by the Real Estate Brokerage Managers Council.

Building a Business for the 21st Century

Collins, James C., and Jerry I. Porras. *Built to Last, Successful Habits of Visionary Companies,* New York: HarperCollins, 1995.

Davidow, William H., and Bro Uttal. *Total Customer Service.* New York: Harper and Row, 1989.

Goleman, Daniel. *Emotional Intelligence.* New York: Bantam Books, 1995.

LeBouef, Michael. *How to Win Customers and Keep Them for Life.* New York: Berkley, 1989.

Spector, Robert, and Patrick D. McCarthy. *The Nordstrom Way.* John Wiley & Sons, Inc., 1995.

REALTOR® Trends

The Home Buying and Selling Process, National Association of REALTORS®, 1994.

Real Estate Brokerage: Income, Expenses, Profits, National Association of REALTORS®, 1995.

Educational Resources

Certified Real Estate Broker (CRB). A REALTOR® designation earned through completing a comprehensive series of one-day courses, focusing on the various aspects of real estate management, including the latest management techniques applied to real estate. For information on the courses and designation, write to the Real Estate Brokerage Managers Council, 430 N. Michigan Ave., Chicago, IL 60611, or call 800-323-0248.

Certified Residential Specialist (CRS). A REALTOR® designation earned through completing a series of sales courses, any three of which provide partial qualification to earn the CRS designation. For information on the courses and the designation, write to the Residential Sales Council, 430 N. Michigan Ave., Chicago, IL 60611, or call 800-462-8841.

Index
